D1535917

Music

as a Way of Knowing

NICK PAGE

Stenhouse Publishers

The Galef Institute

Strategies for Teaching and Learning Professional Library

Administrators: Supporting School Change by Robert Wortman
Assessment: Continuous Learning by Lois Bridges
Creating Your Classroom Community by Lois Bridges
Drama as a Way of Knowing by Paul G. Heller
Math as a Way of Knowing by Susan Ohanian
Music as a Way of Knowing by Nick Page

Look for announcements of future titles in this series on dance, second language learners, literature, physical education, science, visual arts, and writing.

Stenhouse Publishers
The Galef Institute

Library of Congress Cataloging-in-Publication Data
Page, Nick
      Music as a way of knowing : different ways of knowing / by Nick Page.
        p.   cm. — (Strategies for teaching and learning professional library)
      Includes bibliographical references (p.).
      ISBN 1-57110-052-0 (alk. paper)
      1. Music—Instruction and study—Juvenile.   2. School music—Instruction and study—Juvenile.   3. Child development.
      I. Series.
      MT1.P234 1996
      780'.7—dc20
                                          96-45950
                                           CIP

Manufactured in the United States of America on acid-free paper
09 08 07 06 05 04 03 02   8 7 6

Dear Colleague,

This is an exciting time for us to be educators.

Research across disciplines informs our understanding of human learning and development. We know how to support students as active, engaged learners in our classrooms. We know how to continuously assess student learning and development to make sensitive, instructional decisions. This is the art of teaching—knowing how to respond effectively at any given moment to our students' developmental needs.

As educators, we know that learning the art of teaching takes time, practice, and lots of professional support. To that end, the Strategies for Teaching and Learning Professional Library was developed. Each book invites you to explore theory (to know why) in the context of exciting teaching strategies (to know how) connected to evaluation of your students' learning as well as your own (to know you know). In addition, you'll find in-depth information about the unique rigors and challenges of each discipline, to help you make the most of the rich learning and teaching opportunities each discipline offers.

> Use the books' *Dialogues* on your own and in the study groups to reflect upon your practices. The Dialogues invite responses to self-evaluative questions, experimentation with new instructional strategies in classrooms, and perhaps a rethinking of learning philosophy and classroom practices stimulated by new knowledge and understanding.

> *Shoptalks* offer you lively reviews of the best and latest professional literature including professional journals and associations.

> *Teacher-To-Teacher Field Notes* are full of tips and experiences from practicing educators who offer different ways of thinking about teaching practices and a wide range of classroom strategies they've found practical and successful.

As you explore and reflect on teaching and learning, we believe you'll continue to refine and extend your teaching art, and enjoy your professional life and the learning lives of your students.

Here's to the art of teaching!

Lois Bridges
Professional Development Editorial Director,
The Galef Institute

The Strategies for Teaching and Learning Professional Library is part of the Galef Institute's school reform initiative *Different Ways of Knowing*.

Different Ways of Knowing is a philosophy of education based on research in child development, cognitive theory, and multiple intelligences. It offers teachers, administrators, specialists, and other school and district educators continuing professional growth opportunities integrated with teaching and learning materials. The materials are supportive of culturally and linguistically diverse school populations and help all teachers and children to be successful. Teaching strategies focus on interdisciplinary, thematic instruction integrating history and social studies with the performing and visual arts, literature, writing, math, and science. Developed with the leadership of Senior Author Linda Adelman, *Different Ways of Knowing* has been field tested in hundreds of classrooms across the country.

For more information, write or call

The Galef Institute
11050 Santa Monica Boulevard, Third Floor, Los Angeles, California 90025
Tel 310.479.8883
Fax 310.473.9720

Strategies for Teaching and Learning Professional Library

Contributors

President
Linda Adelman

Vice President Programs and Communications
Sue Beauregard

Professional Development Editorial Director
Lois Bridges

Editor
Resa Gabe Nikol

Editorial Assistants
Elizabeth Finison, Wendy Sallin,
Christine DeBoer

Designers
Melvin Harris, Delfina Marquez-Noé,
Sarah McCormick, Jennifer Swan Myers,
Julie Suh

Photographers
Ted Beauregard, Dana Ross

Thanks to Bisse Bowman, primary teacher at Cambridge Friends School in Cambridge, Massachusetts, who has shown me the energy children create through composing their own music, and also for photographing me for this book. Thanks also to Kathy Fiveash, Nancy Langstaff, and Marty Swisher. —NP

Special thanks to Andrew G. Galef and Bronya Pereira Galef for their continuing commitment to our nation's children and educators.

Contents

Chapter 1

Why Music in the Classroom?

Imagine there was no music in the world. No one sang. No one played instruments. No one listened to beautiful melodies or danced to powerful rhythms. Everyone devoted his or her time towards logic, mathematics, reading, writing, science. All forms of play would have to be outlawed, because play and music arise from the same basic instinct—to create, to express, to experiment, to be alive! It is no coincidence that music is of central importance in so many cultures of the world. To many, music is not just an important part of life—music is life itself. Music is alive and by singing and creating sounds we become more alive.

"That's great, but I'm not a musician. I'm afraid of doing music with my students." What is there to be afraid of? In many cultures, everyone participates. There is no separation between talented and untalented. In the Western world, however, we perceive a huge gap—a gap of our own invention. We are all talented. If you can play, you can make music. Like they say in Zimbabwe, "If you can talk, you can sing. If you can walk, you can dance."

You don't need to play an instrument to use music in the classroom. You don't need to know how to read music. You don't need to know who Beethoven was or when the baroque period was. What do you need? You need to be alive. That's it. That is the basic requirement for being musical. You also need to trust your abilities as well as the abilities of your students.

As children, we may have been asked to mouth the words of songs or been told we couldn't play an instrument. Nonsense! Everyone can sing and sing well, and everyone can learn to play an instrument.

Music Is Play

Once there was a teacher who didn't have time to play. "Too busy," she would say. "No time to play. I have to correct the math tests and prepare the test on clouds." I said, "Do you ever play with your students?" "Certainly not," she replied as she quickly disappeared. I peeked into her classroom later that day and caught her doing puppets with the children.

We all play. We all improvise. When we chat informally with our family and friends, we are being spontaneous. We think of speech as being easy, but creating music as being challenging. If you simply get rid of the fears, creating and improvising music can be just as easy as carrying on a conversation. Music is communication. Music is play. And most importantly, music is for all of us, not just the specialists.

D I A L O G U E

What kinds of music do I identify with?

_____

_____

What kinds of music help to define who I am?

_____

_____

What kinds of music help to define the identities of individual students in my classroom?

_____

_____

_____

This book gives you simple first steps for using music across the curriculum. There are three essential reasons music belongs in every classroom.

- Music belongs to all children, not just a few.
- Music supports learning.
- Music builds personal and cultural identity—music builds community.

Once upon a time, not so long ago, everyone sang and everyone made music. Children sang at school and on their way home from school. Musicians made music at local stores or on street corners. Families gathered and made music together. This was before television, a decline in the folk arts, and the invented notion that there are those among us who have no talent or who can't carry a tune.

It's a shame music is cut from so many school budgets. It is also a shame that schools fortunate enough to have music specialists tend to emphasize the few students considered as talented, while the majority of students receive only a passing familiarity with music.

No Separation Between Talented and Untalented

In most parts of the world there is no separation between talented and untalented. Everyone has musical ability. All children should have ample opportunity to express themselves through music, to think through music, and to find themselves through music. Every classroom should be a musical environment.

All children should have ample opportunity to express themselves through music, to think through music, and to find themselves through music.

Music Charges the Brain

New research in the field of learning is showing what ancient cultures have known all along—that music is much more than recreational filler. Music brings brain power! Music strengthens attention spans, aids memory, and provides creative outlets. Music is good for us—it's good for our brains, our bodies, and our spirits.

Beginning in the womb, a child is surrounded by sound. Of the five senses, the ears are the most active before birth. Only the shortest hairs of the cochlea have developed at this stage, providing the fetus the ability to hear only the highest of sounds, primarily the percussive consonants of words. The phrase "percussive consonance" would be heard only as *Pe—Ku—Ss—fv Ko—Ss—nSs*. Low sounds like the heart are felt, but not heard. Floating in water, the fetus bathes in the sounds of parents' voices and surrounding sounds. Just as the umbilical cord is providing nutrients for the child to grow physically, the sounds provide needed resonance for the mind to grow.

The ear has three purposes, not two. It is now believed that in addition to balance and hearing, the ear also serves as a charger for the brain. The desire to learn is equated with the desire to listen. Listening is a skill of great importance. The child who no longer desires to listen, no longer desires to learn. The musical child, however, develops a hunger for listening and learning equal to a hunger for nutrition.

As will be discussed later, the ability to hear sounds silently in the head is an essential skill for children, particularly in their transition to silent reading.

There is a rhythm in our reading, rhythms in our math solving tasks, and rhythms in our basic attention span.

Field Notes: Teacher-To-Teacher

I knew a girl once who claimed she couldn't sing in tune. "Nonsense," I would say, "everyone can sing in tune." "Nope," she would insist, "I can't sing a note."

I asked her how she knew this. "Brother told me. Sister told me. Friends told me."

I sang a soft "Oo" vowel and asked her to hear it in her head. "Yeah, so?" she responded.

"Can you hear it?" I asked. She could. "Sing it," I said. She sang the note and it was perfectly in tune. I smiled and told her her friends were wrong.

–NP

There Are Rhythms in Learning

Along with hearing the sound internally, feeling the pulse internally is also essential. It is now believed that there is a rhythm to learning. There is a rhythm in our reading, rhythms in our math solving tasks, and rhythms in our basic attention span. Those children who can sustain a pulse can also sustain their attention. Rhythms of reading and problem solving become more fluid with the help of musical activities.

There is a little known phenomenon in nature called *entrainment*. Entrainment, quite simply, is the tendency for one pulse to imitate another pulse. Kindergarten teachers are often aware that the speed of their speech and actions will affect their children. Children may imitate hyperactivity and become hyper themselves. Teachers who speak slowly to children receive calm reactions. Our rhythms copy each other. Two people walking down the street will often begin to walk in the same rhythm.

Biologists note that everything from heart rates to brain waves entrain to other rhythms. A car mechanic entrains the engine when he or she tunes it. Examples of entrainment are all around us.

It is possible to use musical activities as simple as clapping or marching to create powerful learning environments where an entire class becomes "in sync" with itself. Students may become unified in the rhythm, able to learn at an accelerated pace.

Every day in the life of a child has its own rhythms. Using entrainment, you can smooth out the transitions between one activity and another. You can use a song to ease children into quiet reading. You can use music as a signal for meeting time. You can insert a song during a sleepy afternoon math class to simply wake the students up and charge their brains.

As I have said, everything from brain waves to heartbeats to breathing can be entrained using music. It is a powerful tool, one worth recognizing.

Music Is Good for Memory

The ability to sequence activities or thoughts and retain them is a necessary learning skill. Because of entrainment and the rhythms of learning, it is easier for a child to learn a song or rap than it is to learn a history lesson or math table. The brain seems to work musically—learning with the aid of music becomes almost effortless. It is no coincidence that so many of us learned the alphabet through "The Alphabet Song."

S H O P T A L K

Brewer, Chris and Don G. Campbell. *Rhythms of Learning: Creative Tools for Developing Lifelong Skills*. Tucson, Arizona: Zephyr Press, 1991.
This book presents interesting views on rhythm and how to use rhythmic awareness in teaching. It discusses subjects like entrainment and provides examples.

Lazear, David. *Seven Pathways of Learning: Teaching Students and Parents about Multiple Intelligences*. Tucson, Arizona: Zephyr Press, 1994.
This is one of four excellent books by Lazear using Howard Gardner's approach to the seven intelligences.

Institute for Music, Health, and Education. Don G. Campbell, Director, P.O. Box 1244, Boulder, Colorado 80306.
The Institute is dedicated to the research of listening and its uses in health and education. The Institute distributes many books and tapes including information on accelerated learning.

Music = Creativity = Play

The act of making music, whether singing a song or composing a piece for pencil sharpeners and sandpaper, is a creative act. Creativity is play and both of these elements are essential for learning. Improvising is something children do all the time. Recess, for example, is a grand drama enacted every day featuring armies drumming into battle, mothers singing to their young, and legions of chanting jump ropers. You can bring this musical play into the classroom.

When we create something—a work of art or a song—we are being compassionate. We are making the world a more beautiful place by giving of ourselves. And the wellspring of this creativity is the same source as all creativity in the universe. Galaxies create planets and suns. Children create songs and dances. Each makes the world better. In Western Africa, the act of making music is synonymous with the act of giving. The main reason for making music is to be generous. Creativity is born of our generosity of spirit.

SHOPTALK

Nash, Grace C. and Janice Rapley. *Music in the Making: Optimal Learning in Speech, Song, Instrument Instruction, and Movement for Grades K-4.* Van Nuys, California: Alfred Publishing, 1990.

Grace Nash revolutionized music education during the 50s and 60s. Her books on counting and reading rhythm games are excellent for classroom teachers. Look for *Do It My Way: The Child's Way of Learning* and *Creative Approaches to Child Development*, also published by Alfred Publishing. Check your school library for older editions of her books.

A Musical Class Is a Disciplined Class

All of us, children and adults, need to feel a sense of self-worth. We enjoy the power achieved through a strong identity. Unfortunately, children are often denied this power because of educational systems that rely on authoritarian discipline. When children are denied power or a sense of self-worth, they will create it for themselves—they will seek power in whatever ways they can. A cigarette brings power. A knife or gun brings power.

But music also brings power, a power stronger than any gun. Children are born with this power. When given the opportunity to shine with all their might through music and through the arts, children don't need the negative powers available in society. For cultures all around the planet, the expression of music is the expression of self. When an individual makes music, he or she is saying, "This is my power. This is who I am. No one can take this from me." When a group sings, they become as powerful as stars, not a destructive hierarchical power where self-worth depends on being better than someone else, but a living power where self-worth depends on the interdependence of all.

There was once a teacher who would yell, "Line up!" She'd keep yelling until everyone had lined up several minutes later. In the next classroom, the teacher would sing, "Clean up time." Her students would immediately echo back, "Clean up time." She'd sing, "Line up time," and the class would echo, singing, "Line up time." And in the background, you could hear the teacher in the next room yelling, yelling, yelling to her students who had stopped listening a long time ago.

Music-Making Builds Community

Children's first songs are about objects and activities in their immediate world. They become part of the songs. They find identity in the songs. The words "I" and "me" are in all the great children's songs. When the song "Twinkle, Twinkle, Little Star" says, "How I wonder what you are," it is the child who wonders. The chorus to Raffi's song, "Baby Beluga," ends with, "Is your Mama home with you so happy?" These are comforting words. A song about a whale becomes a song about themselves.

As a child's world expands, the subject matter of his or her songs expands. Songs about "we" and "them" become acceptable. The child's world is growing along with his or her identity.

Long ago, each tribe or cultural group had its own musical identity. As our tribes and cultures have mixed together, we no longer have one kind of music to identify with. A child today has a panorama of cultural styles. The child can identify with heavy metal, rap, hip-hop, folk, soul, European classical, oldies rock and roll, gospel, country, pop, punk, blues, jazz, plus all the cultural styles of music from Africa, Europe, Asia, Latin America, and Native America. We are multicultural, whether we know it or not.

S H O P T A L K

Sleeter, Christine E. and Carl A. Grant. *Making Choices for Multicultural Education: Five Approaches to Race, Class, and Gender.* Columbus, Ohio: Merrill Publishing, 1988.

This excellent book gives the history of the multicultural movement in education, from the period of the rising African American awareness to the current movement towards inclusiveness and the democratization of education.

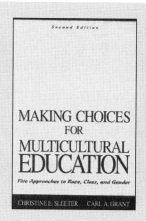

The learning environment that embraces diversity is a healthy place. Teachers who openly show their dislike for rap, rock, or country show through example that diversity is unacceptable. Teachers who accept all musical styles convey a positive message. You may not identify with the music yourself, but you have to allow others to identify with the music if they choose. It is that choice that is part of the child's expanding identity. We want children to grow up in accepting environments where differences between people and their behaviors are celebrated, not ignored or torn apart.

DIALOGUE

When does my school have celebrations where students can sing and make music with each other?

_____

_____

How would all-school singing celebrations help my students and the entire school community?

_____

_____

_____

Group singing and music-making help to build strong classroom learning communities.

When we, as teachers, introduce the music of diverse cultures, we expand the child's world. But there is more. When a class gathers to sing or make music, they are doing something quite ancient and powerful. Group singing is a communal form of play, a joyful ritual bringing everyone together. A different kind of identity arises—a group identity, a group spirit. This feeling of camaraderie is vital for the powerful learning environment. The student who feels a powerful connection with the rest of the learning community will also find a powerful connection to the process of learning itself. Group singing and music-making help to build strong classroom learning communities. When this community music-making is shared in school assemblies and performances for families and friends, tremendous celebrations are created—celebrations of how truly magnificent we are.

Field Notes: Teacher-To-Teacher

I scheduled a family sing-along at my school for a Friday evening. Some parents came to me and complained that the show disrupted their TV time.

I said, "If you want a show, stay home and watch TV. If you want to celebrate, come join us."

—NP

To conclude, all the elements of music are needed in a learning environment.

- We need sound to charge the brain.
- We need inner hearing for reading and problem solving.
- We need prolonged rhythms to prolong our attention spans.
- We need song learning to aid in memory skills.
- We need music as a form of play.
- We need music to help define who we are and, particularly, how great we are.

DIALOGUE

As an exploration of multiple intelligences, listen to a recording of your choice and then think about how you would represent the music through writing, symbols, movement, song, drawing, drama, play.

Now choose two ways and describe the piece of music.

_____

_____

_____

_____

_____

For further exploration, do the same activity with colleagues and then let students show you what they can do!

Chapter 2

How To Write Songs and Raps

Many of the specific musical activities that I suggest to accompany your math, reading, writing, science, social studies, and history curriculum require creativity on the part of both you and your students. We are constantly improvising through our speech and actions. It is only a small step to the level of writing songs and raps. Trust your creativity and the creativity of your students.

Your Musical Ingredients

We should never be too analytical about music, breaking it down into too many parts, because the process of analysis may kill some of the magic. As in biology, we can take living things apart, but we cannot give them life. It is helpful to know the musical terms I introduce here, but alone they do not make up music. Music is a living spirit that sings from all of us (if we trust it).

Form. As in poetry, form refers to the order of sections. For example, the phrase "Twinkle, twinkle, little star, / How I wonder what you are" can be called theme a^1. "Up above the world so high" is theme b^1 and "like a diamond in the sky" is b^2 because it is the same melody as b^1 but stated for the second time. Similarly, the last phrase, "Twinkle, twinkle, little star, / How I wonder what you are" would be theme a^2. The form of "Twinkle, Twinkle, Little Star" would then be $a^1b^1b^2a^2$ or abba.

Longer pieces like symphonies use grand forms with the works broken up into four movements, each with its own A and B themes. Capital letters are used to symbolize longer themes. If we were to make a medley of "Twinkle, Twinkle, Little Star" and the song "Star Light, Star Bright," we might call "Twinkle, Twinkle" the A theme and "Star Light, Star Bright" the B theme. It would sound nice in an ABA form. In creating musical forms, remember that themes repeat, and it is the order of this repetition that largely determines the form of a musical selection.

To understand the concept of form better, you can sit down and listen to familiar pieces and determine their forms. Ask yourself, what is the difference between the form of a spiritual like "This Little Light of Mine" and a hymn like "Amazing Grace." Listen to a European classical work and listen for the two main contrasting themes, A and B. Then listen to what happens to these themes. The first movement of Beethoven's *Fifth Symphony*, for example, has startlingly different A and B themes, and he develops or improvises on them in ingenious ways. This is the piece with the familiar four-note motif that everyone calls, "Da da da dah!" Listen and learn how those four notes are repeated over and over again.

Now listen to music from a country like Ghana and hear how radically the forms differ. Oftentimes, the music of other cultures is organized quite differently from ours. For example, in contrast to our verse-chorus song structures, Ghanaian drumming involves layers of rhythms that change according to signals given by a leader.

Of all the musical elements, form is the most interesting. Repetition is key to all form and music. Don't be afraid of creating a piece of music, whether you sing it or play it with handmade instruments, that uses different contrasting themes, played both simultaneously and one after the other. Have fun with form.

Dynamics. It is fun to play with volume—with how loud or soft the music is. While singing a song or playing a piece, try making the music gradually grow louder or softer. You don't need to use terms like *crescendo* to have fun with dynamics.

Rhythm and pulse. Similarly, you can play with the speed or pulse of a piece. How does speeding up the tempo or pulse change the feeling of a song or piece? How does slowing it down make a difference?

You don't need to know what a quarter note is to understand rhythm. Say the phrase, "Row, row, row your boat." Now compare it with the phrase, "Merrily, merrily, merrily, merrily." By speaking them, you can see that they have two distinct rhythms with a pulse that remains the same for both. We are constantly putting words into rhythms. "Hello, how are you?" has its own rhythm, as does the phrase, "I'm fine, what's that on your tie?"

The rhythm of words is a simple way to approach musical rhythms. With your students, you can say, "Hello, how are you?" then have them say and clap the rhythm, then just clap the rhythm. Next try the rhythm on instruments.

Jazzy rhythms are called *syncopated*. Children have no problem doing seemingly difficult syncopated or jazzy rhythms, especially in these days of rap and hip-hop. As with all rhythms, it is important to keep the pulse steady. Experiment with a spoken phrase like "Alligators ate my lunch today." There are millions of rhythms you can use. Try making them plain and dull, then try making them jazzy and syncopated. Hold some vowels out for a long time like, "A-a-a-l-li-gators a-a-a-a-a-te my lunch."

When your students begin to write their own songs and raps, feel free to explore the many rhythmic possibilities.

Melody. When words are sung, they become melodies. Any sequence of pitches, whether sung or played, becomes a melody. You don't need to know that the name of the notes may be D, E, F#, E, and A. Nor do you need to know how to read or write notes on a music staff. If you can sing a melody, then you can compose a melody.

You do need to know what a scale is. The Rodgers and Hammerstein song, "Do-Re-Mi," uses the notes Do, Re, Mi, Fa, So, La, Ti, with Do repeated at the end. Sung in sequence from the lowest pitch to the highest pitch, you create a scale—eight notes with the first and last notes being the same note. The scale in this song is the *major* scale; the *minor* scale would be the same sequence of notes, but starting on La (A).

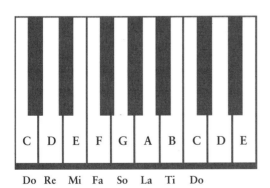

Do Re Mi Fa So La Ti Do

The word *octave* describes the distance between the first and last notes of our Western scales or between any pitched note and the next note with the same name, eight notes higher or lower. Eight notes above F sharp (F#) is F sharp again—an octave. (See how simple all this is?)

When you begin to compose melodies, you 'll want to use the eight notes in one of the scales. There are five other possible notes that fall between the scale notes (sharps and flats), but it is not necessary to worry about these. Most of the folksongs we sing use the eight main notes of the Western scales. We all hear these scales quite naturally.

Timbre. A string on an instrument vibrates and creates a pitch. The violin, guitar, and piano all use strings, but each sounds very different from the other. They have different timbres or tone qualities. An orchestra is made of many diverse timbres, each unique. All children have different sounding voices. They have different timbres. The sound of a ruler dropping onto a desk has a different timbre than the sound of a ruler being rubbed against the surface of the desk. Make a diving board with a ruler at the edge of a desk, then pluck it, making a delightful *boiiing* sound. There are dozens of variations on this timbre that you can make depending on how far the ruler sticks out. (You are also changing the pitch—the more ruler surface on the desk, the lower in pitch the *boiiing* is going to be.)

Timbres are fun to play with. You can be very creative with the different sound qualities that even one instrument can make. For example, turn your hands into tuned drums. Clap your hands using cup-shaped palms, then clap using flat palms. The pitches and timbres are different. Now snap your fingers and rub your hands together. These are just four of the many timbres you can make with your hands.

Harmony. Whenever two or more pitches are sounded or sung at the same time, a harmony is created. Western harmony is based on *triads*, three note chords. Most triads consist of the first, third, and fifth notes in the scale sung at the same time (or second, fourth, and sixth, etc.). You don't need to use harmony when you are composing; but it's nice to know it's there, especially if you end up composing a round. It is good to know about harmony when you lead songs.

Texture. When you combine multiple sounds (melodies, rhythms, timbres), you create a musical texture. The many different timbres in an orchestra create a wonderful texture as do the interweaving melodies of rounds sung by children. Any time you combine different timbres, dynamics, or melodies, you create textures. The combined texture is always more interesting than any of its parts. A singing voice sounds lovely as does a flute playing the same note, but both at the same time create an even more beautiful texture.

We are surrounded by textures of sound. The combined sounds of children at recess—yelling, singing, and running—is a rich texture. The sounds of commuter traffic can be an annoying texture. Musical textures are simply the combination of different sounds.

Creating the Creative Environment

Nothing stops a child's creativity like a negative comment. A class is writing the words for a song. Joey makes a suggestion; others reject his ideas. In brainstorming sessions, it is essential that all ideas be accepted. Once a child like Joey has experienced rejection, he is likely to turn off his creative output, as will others afraid of similar criticism. A creative environment is one where everyone has a say. Both teacher and students need constant support in order for the creative environment to work. With support, children's creativity can truly sparkle.

SHOPTALK

Fink, Cathy, Marcy Marxer, Robin Williams and Linda Williams. *Learn To Sing Harmony.* Woodstock, New York: Homespun Tapes, 1986.

Audiotapes with booklet. *Learn To Sing Harmony* is good for the beginner, although it's no substitute for joining a chorus or folk-song group and experiencing harmony firsthand.

In a creative environment, everyone makes suggestions and gets support from the group.

Writing Songs and Raps

There are five simple steps to composing songs or raps, beginning with choosing a topic followed by a brainstorming session. In the next two steps, you write the words and the rhythm, then create a melody or in the case of a rap, the background rhythm. The final step is the revision process.

But first, you have to figure out a way of remembering what you have composed once you are finished. There are two ways of doing this, the simplest being to record the rhythms and melodies on a tape recorder. The other way is to write the words, rhythms, and melodies in a manner that works for you. Rhythms are easily graphed, showing long and short notes as well as long and short pauses between notes or syllables (rests). Accents above syllables are very helpful as are bar lines (/) between phrases. Melodies can be shown by their shape as you will see in a moment. It is easy to write songs, but it is also easy to forget them afterwards, so it's important to have a system for remembering them.

Step 1—Identify the theme or topic. It's important that everyone writing the song focus on the theme or topic of the song. You can begin with a simple discussion or by writing ideas on the board.

Step 2—Brainstorm. Let's say the class wants to write a song about butterflies. They have studied caterpillars, cocoons, and butterflies. They know words like *chrysalis* and *metamorphosis*.

Write down students' word phrase ideas on the board or on newsprint. Remember to keep things very positive. Avoid negativity. A student suggests the word "changes." You record it. Someone else suggests, "changes, changes changes" and someone else says "changes, changes, changes, a metamorphosis."

Another student suggests that the phrase works as a repeating refrain. Then someone suggests the line, "Caterpillars eat leaves." You write the idea down. Someone else says, "Once upon a time there was a caterpillar named Bill." You record it. Eventually, students may choose to drop these ideas, but you'll want to accept all suggestions. Someone else picks up on the last suggestion and says, "Its name should be Caterpillarella, like Cinderella." Everyone agrees.

You continue like this, keeping the energy high, and recording every suggestion. What form should the song take? Should certain lines repeat? Remember that it is the order of repetition that determines form. You may end up with lines like "Caterpillarella with a hundred legs" or one-word phrases like "cocoon," with the second syllable held out.

S H O P T A L K

Stanley, Lawrence A., ed. *Rap, the Lyrics: The Words to Rap's Greatest Hits*. New York: Penguin Books, 1992.

From urban poetry to angry political statements, this collection of rap lyrics is a valuable source for anyone who wants to know more about rap. Understanding leads to appreciation.

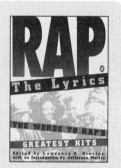

Step 3—Create the words and rhythm. As they brainstorm, students will suggest many word phrases. Keep encouraging them. What else? What else? Keep the ideas flowing. Remind them of the theme and topic. What else changes like the butterfly? A student suggests that we change, but not in the same way. Another student says, "I'd rather be a butterfly than a caterpillar." You record it. Eventually a student says, "We all get second chances to be like the butterfly." Another student suggests using that line then moving into the "changes, changes" line. Everyone agrees.

Once you have lots of ideas, you begin to put them together. This happens slowly. Eventually a rough order of phrases evolves. You then discuss different rhythms. What syllables should be held? Which should go quickly? Should some phrases be fast and others slow? When should the rhythm be plain and when can it have syncopation? Should it be like a waltz (in three beats) or like a march (in four beats)? This may be enough to work on in one session.

Step 4—Creating melodies or background beats. Composing a melody is not as hard as it may sound. First, you have to know that all melodies have shapes. Some are ascending lines, some are descending. With the students, sing the melody for "Twinkle, Twinkle, Little Star." As they sing, have them shape the contour of the melody with their hands. The a¹ theme, "Twinkle, twinkle, little star, / How I wonder what you are," is in the shape of an arch. Sing other melodies and discuss their shapes. Try "Row, Row, Row Your Boat," and "Happy Birthday to You." Notice how the shapes themselves tend to repeat, although differently. This, remember, is called musical form.

When students understand the concept of melodic shape, begin creating shapes to the melodies. The rhythms you have created may change as you do this, and that's okay. Take the phrase, "Caterpillarella, with a hundred legs." Ask the students what shape would work well with those words. Someone suggests a straight line. You try it. Someone else suggests a wave. You try that and other suggestions. Everyone finally agrees on a bowl-shape melody. You go on to the next phrase. They decide to use the same shape but with different notes.

Revising and editing songs provides an excellent opportunity for children to work collaboratively.

Does this sound too sophisticated for children? It's not. Making up melodies is natural for them. The most natural melody is the the "Na Na" taunt melody. Whole songs can be written using those three notes G, E, and A.

Step 5—Revising and editing. The final step of making improvements and polishing the song can be as challenging as the first steps of creating the song. It's important to be critical without being destructive. It is also important that no one working on the song be inflexible regarding changes. This is an excellent opportunity to learn how to work collaboratively.

If you did not begin by focusing in on the subject or theme of the song, time could be wasted in this final stage with students arguing about what the song should be about. Remembering that first stage during the polishing process, therefore, is extremely important. Does the finished song say what the group meant it to say? What changes can be made to make it fit the theme or topic better?

Maybe the song you have written says something completely different, but everyone still likes it. That's okay, too. Keep it.

An important thing to remember while working on the song with your students is that the process works. Trust it, or it won't work. Things may fall apart. But when the ideas start flying, the process is truly amazing. It's like watching the creative evolution of nature, but sped up to a breathtaking speed.

The results might not be as well crafted as a Lerner and Loewe song and it might not make the top ten like a Motown classic, but the song will belong to your students. To them, it will be a #1 hit.

If you are making the song into a rap, you may want to create a background rhythm as accompaniment. Try a repeated spoken phrase like "Cater, Cater…Caterpillarella, Cater, Cater…Caterpillarella." Say the name quickly and repeat the "Cater" fragments in slow steady pulses. Or make it syncopated. Then transfer that spoken rhythm to either claps or instruments. I have seen students doing a great background beat using simply the bottom and sides of a plastic trash can. Using the low-cupped clap and the high-slap clap, you can create great beats. If you happen to have access to electronic sequencers, samplers, or drum machines, you can also create exciting rap and hip-hop backgrounds.

If you are unfamiliar with rap and hip-hop, read *Rap Attack 2: African Rap to Global Hip Hop* by David Toop. There are also books available that offer the lyrics to many popular rap songs. I have heard the argument that rap isn't music. My response is that every culture defines music differently and that music helps to define each culture. When you understand how rap evolved, you see that it comes from one of the oldest musical traditions on earth. It is music of tremendous power. As Quincy Jones says, rap is here to stay.

S H O P T A L K

Toop, David. *Rap Attack 2: African Rap to Global Hip Hop.* London: Serpent's Tail, 1991.

Here's an eye-opening look at the history of rap music from its African roots, to its Jamaican and New York merger, to its latest commercialization. It's a short book, but it says a lot about the music and culture of urban America.

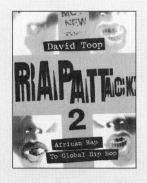

Wiggins, Jackie. *Composition in the Classroom: A Tool for Teaching.* Reston, Virginia: Music Educators National Conference (MENC), 1991.

Here's a good how-to book with fun examples of songs and compositions by elementary school students.

When the song is complete and polished, be sure to record it. Display the words so everyone can look at them with both pride and with a sense of ownership. If possible, perform the piece for family members, for other classes, or for the school.

Here is a song written by the first- and second-grade students of Bisse Bowman's class in Cambridge, Massachusetts. It is from the opera they wrote called *Wicked and the Devil,* based on an Appalachian folktale. A farmer named John has led a wicked life. When he dies, they won't let him into heaven, so he tries to get into hell.

Wicked John Ain't Comin' Down Here

The Creative Act Is Not Complete Until It Is Shared

A father asked his son what it felt like to sing a solo in front of the whole school. The boy replied, "I liked being ten feet tall."

Every year, Bisse Bowman's first- and second-grade students compose their own opera. They choose their favorite story read to them during the year. With Bowman's help they compose the songs, one for each main scene. The whole class sings these simple songs without piano accompaniment. Bowman selects the lead characters who sing all their own dialogue, something remarkably easy for a six year old to do. During the two week period of writing and rehearsing the play, the students' academic work actually improves because their attention level is so highly charged by their work on the opera. The performance of these operas is always the high point of the school year. It is both delightful and fascinating.

Composing With Computers

There are many sophisticated music software programs available for professional composers. Music programs for children are often geared towards music reading and music history. There are, however, some simple and amazing programs that allow children to compose exciting music with little or no instruction.

A good place to begin is with a sequencer. Many companies make toy sequencers that are inexpensive, simple to use, and fairly versatile. It is easy,  for example, to program a background drum beat or a background harmony. On many of these sequencers all you have to do is press C to get a three note C major chord. Press another button and the chord is played in a rock beat pattern or whatever rhythm you choose. Some of the less expensive sequencers also "sample." You can sample your own voice. The machine records your voice, for example, singing the sound "ah." Then when you press any note on the keyboard, you will hear your voice. You can have fun sampling ordinary sounds and creating musical pieces.

Most software programs require the use of a Musical Instrument Digital Interface (MIDI). A MIDI is an electric keyboard that is able to support computers. With most MIDI software, you can play notes on the electric piano (MIDI) and have the notes appear on the computer monitor. You can then program the computer to play the music back to you. To hear the music, you will also need either earphones or an amplifier with speakers. This equipment is not inexpensive.

If your school has an Apple II computer or better, there are fun software packages that require no MIDI or amplification system. You can compose right at the computer using the mouse. You can then hear the music you composed played through the computer's speakers.

Perhaps the fastest growing computer music phenomenon is the world of CD-ROMs. If your school's computers can support CD-ROMs, there are programs available for the study of music that are quite amazing. You can see and hear an orchestra playing Beethoven's *Ninth Symphony*. Press a button and you can hear commentary on the symphony or a biography of the composer. There are programs available that mix math, social studies, and music in powerful learning activities. They will be terrific aids for the integration of the arts into all learning.

With a modem, you can communicate through the Internet and many other computer message services as you would with a telephone at a fraction of the cost. Already, it is possible to buy music through the computer modem. Soon you will be able to call a company and see and hear a piece of music that you're thinking of ordering. After you decide what you want and type the order—presto—it will print out on your printer.

Like everything in the computer industry, music software packages are constantly being eliminated, upgraded, or made available for other systems. Below are some suggested resources to help you investigate computerized music further.

The three most popular hardware systems for music are the Apple, Atari, and IBM-compatible computers. There are good programs for all three, but they aren't compatible with each other, so you'll want to get the software for the computer your school has, or for the computer with which you can expand. Of the three, Atari is currently the only system with a built-in interface between the computer and the MIDI. With the other two you have to buy a MIDI interface.

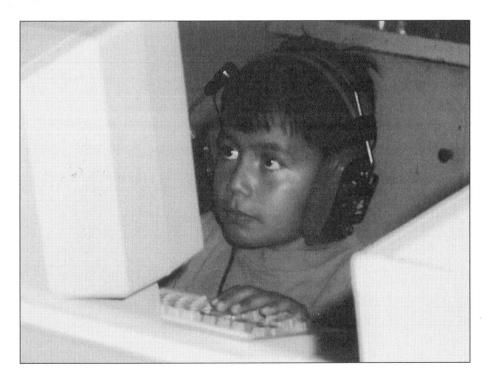

Music and Computer Resources
Alexander Publishing. 3537 Old Conejo Road, Suite 101, Newberry Park, California 91320. They publish manuals giving simple explanations on how to use the many MIDI systems and electric pianos. (The original instructions tend to be incomprehensible without a degree in computer programming!)

Computers and Music. 647 Mission Street, San Francisco, California 94105. This is a quarterly catalog of current software and hardware, for both Mac and IBM, including educational materials.

Honey Rock. RD 4, Box 87, Everett, Pennsylvania 15537. This company provides multicultural, percussion-related materials for performers and music educators, including how to purchase drums from around the world.

Maestro Music, Inc. 2403 San Mateo NE P-12, Albuquerque, New Mexico 87110. This company writes music theory software for Apple II. The software is aimed at grades 1-12 as a support to music specialists—how to read and understand music.

Micro Music, Inc. 5353 Buford Highway, Atlanta, Georgia 30340. A retailer of music hardware and software, Micro Music sells a book that reviews available music software—*The Musical PC* by MIDI America.

OPCODE, New Tools For Education. 3950 Fabian Way, Palo Alto, California 94303. OPCODE software is very accessible, easy to use. It is MIDI-friendly, meaning that their programs work well with keyboards. They have some powerful software at relatively low prices.

S H O P T A L K

Wiggins, Jackie. *Synthesizers in the Elementary Music Classroom: An Integrated Approach*. Reston, Virginia: Music Educators National Conference (MENC), 1991.

If your school has Atari or Amiga computers, this is a good resource to have. Both computers were designed for excellent music use. A reliable Atari and Amiga music software maker is Dr. T's, 220 Boylston Street, Suite 206, Chestnut Hill, Massachusetts 02167. MENC also publishes *TIPS: Technology for Music Educators* by Charles G. Boody. It gives fun electronic activities for the classroom.

Chapter 3

Music Across the Curriculum

The main purpose of this book is to give you ideas on how to use music in the classroom. I have already discussed composing songs, and the last chapter discusses teaching songs. These are most likely to make up the majority of your musical activities. Certainly, writing and singing songs in the subjects of math, science, art, language arts, geography, history, and social studies will always be worthwhile.

With all the ideas I propose, it's essential that you trust your innate creativity and the creativity of your students. To the painter, the empty canvas is not an image of fear, but an image of possibilities. The possibilities are limitless. The act of creating something from nothing is always the most rewarding act of all.

Music Enhances Reading and Writing

Every child makes a transition between reading out loud and reading silently. When we sing, we do not sing with our mouths only. Our ears are equal partners. Singing is an act of listening and recreating with our voices what we hear. We listen internally—in our heads. Singing with young children strengthens their ability to hear internally, and this is a great aid in the transition towards silent reading—towards the internalization of words.

The fact that singing also uses words is a fantastic bonus. Learning new songs with the aid of large mounted word sheets is a tremendous help in teaching reading. Keeping notebooks or song journals is an excellent activity for children learning to write.

Children can learn letters, vowel sounds, and spelling within the context of songs—whole natural language. Using hand signs, you can lead simple call-and-response activities where you sing an "Oo" vowel while making an "O" shape with your hands. The students echo this. A nursery rhyme like "Hickory Dickery Dock" can become a game for playing with consonants and vowels.

Leader: Hhhhhhhi (Leader motions an H shape with his or her hands.)
Group: Hhhhhhhi (Children echo motion.)
Leader: K! (Shaping a K.)
Group: K!
Leader: Oh!
Group: Oh!
Leader: Rrrrrrry
Group: Rrrrrrry

Anything that strengthens inner hearing also strengthens reading abilities. Music does this.

This activity with simple vowels and consonants aids pronunciation and reading. Try the rhyme again using only the ends of words. Many children tend to cut off the ends of their words. Singing can become a guide to good pronunciation.

It is easy to create spelling songs. Children often retain sung information better than spoken. This is because patterns are easier for the brain to process than random information. Using the call-and-response technique, have students repeat simple sung phrases like "Hat, spelled H-A-T," or

Leader: Lasagna
Group: Lasagna
Leader: Some cats like lasagna
Group: Some cats like lasagna
Leader: All A's with a silent G
Group: All A's with a silent G
Leader: And an S, not a Z
Group: And an S, not a Z
Leader: L-A-S-A-G-N-A
Group: L-A-S-A-G-N-A
Leader: That's yummy yum lasagna
Group: That's yummy yum lasagna

Anything that strengthens inner hearing also strengthens reading abilities. Music does this.

Many educators have begun using background music in the classroom, particularly when students are reading—not rock and roll, but gentler music like folk music from diverse traditions or classical music. The music creates a powerful mind-set related to entrainment, mentioned earlier in this book. The rhythms of the brain imitate the rhythms of the music, enhancing learning and increasing attention span. The music creates a mood—quieting down hyper minds so that some steady concentration can begin.

Bisse Bowman, the teacher whose students compose operas every year, invites her students to select tapes to play before school starts and at other free times during the day. The students take great pride in picking whatever they wish, including all forms of pop music. A good investment for every classroom is a cassette tape recorder that can both play and record music.

D I A L O G U E

What are the transition times during the day when I can lead songs in my classroom?

_____

_____

When can I lead songs in the middle of or as part of an academic learning time?

_____

_____

Music Enhances Mathematics

Research has shown that college students listening to Mozart increased their short-term spatial reasoning (Rauscher, Shaw and Ky 1993). Rauscher, Shaw, Levine, Ky, and Wright at the University of California, Irvine, extended this research in their study "Music and Spatial Task Performance: A Causal Relationship," concluding that three year olds who study music enhance their long-term spatial reasoning (1994). Preschoolers at two different schools who had eight months of keyboard lessons and group singing sessions outperformed children with no musical training at object assembly tasks, which required children to "form a mental image and then orient physical objects to reproduce that image."

Many teachers have already experienced positive results in using music as a tool for teaching mathematics. Through music, students can improve their spatial reasoning, counting, problem solving, graphing, and use and understanding of ratios.

Counting songs have been part of the kindergarten repertoire for many years. Author Grace Nash offers many rhythm games and songs that are invaluable aids in learning to count, add, and multiply (see Chapter 1 Shoptalk on page 12). Even simple call-and-response singing can be used to teach math. For example, the teacher can sing "One apple," (students echo) "and one apple," (echo) "makes two apples" (echo).

Learning to make graphs or diagrams to describe abstract ideas is a helpful problem-solving strategy. Combining this skill with listening can be an even more powerful experience. Listen to a piece of music and invent a graph or other system for writing it down.

Learning to make graphs or diagrams to describe music is a helpful problem-solving strategy.

For example, begin by having the students draw the contour of a melody like "Twinkle, Twinkle, Little Star" or "Row, Row, Row Your Boat." Make it even more accurate on graph paper. Then invite students to create their own melodic shapes on a graph, having them sing them afterwards. Many easy-to-use computer software programs allow students to compose music using graphs rather than the standard five-lined staff system. Technically speaking, the five-line staff system is a graph. Reading music requires math skills. Reading music strengthens math skills.

Here is the song, "Twinkle, Twinkle, Little Star," written in standard five-line staff notation, then as a graph, then in a few other variations.

Twinkle, Twinkle, Little Star

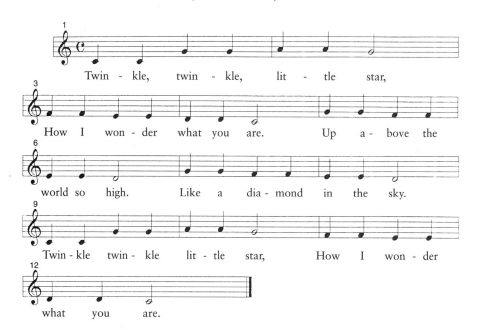

"Twinkle, Twinkle, Little Star" Chart

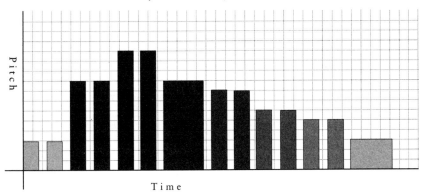

Words

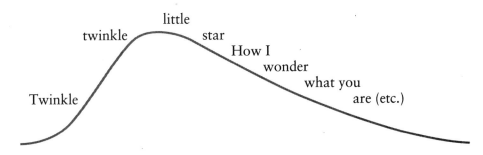

Numbers

1,1,5,5,6,6,5—4,4,3,3,2,2,1—

5,5,4,4,3,3,2—5,5,4,4,3,3,2—

1,1,5,5,6,6,5—4,4,3,3,2,2,1—

Letters

c, c, g, g, a, a, g—f, f, e, e, d, d, c—

g, g, f, f, e, e, d—g, g, f, f, e, e, d—

c, c, g, g, a, a, g—f, f, e, e, d, d, c—

You can have fun with both letters and numbers and make an algebraic formula. (See above)

If $X = 2c+2g+2a+g$

and $Y = 2f+2e+2d+c$

and $Z = 2g+2f+2e+d$

then "Twinkle, Twinkle, Little Star" $= X+Y+2Z+X+Y$

As an advanced version of this exercise, students can listen to a longer piece like Rossini's *William Tell Overture*. Encourage them to invent a system for describing the work's form. They will notice it starts with a long slow section, and that suddenly the "Lone Ranger" theme appears. What else happens? Other fun pieces are Tchaikovsky's *1812 Overture,* or the first movement of Beethoven's *Fifth Symphony*. Don't rely on the European traditions only. Invite students to determine the form to Dave Brubeck's jazz classic "Blue Rondo à la Turk," Baba Olatunji's Nigerian drum classic "Jingo," or a classic doo-wop song like "Earth Angel."

S H O P T A L K

RAPS & RHYMES IN MATHS

Baker, Ann and Johnny Baker. *Raps and Rhymes in Maths*. Portsmouth, New Hampshire: Heinemann, 1991.

Here's a fun collection of math activities which help teachers address areas such as measuring, time, probability, and attitudes toward math for both lower and upper primary classes.

Music and ratios. There are many parallels between music and mathematics. Pythagoras, in ancient Greece, taught that all pitches are the product of frequency ratios. This is a scientific reality. The easiest way to demonstrate this is to lay a guitar on its back and measure the length of its lowest or thickest string. The students can record the length on a graph of their design. Place the fleshy part of a fingertip on the string without pressing down. With the other hand, begin plucking the string as you move the first hand towards the middle of the guitar. Most of the notes won't ring, but suddenly, in the exact middle, a note will ring out. Be sure that you don't press down, simply hold your finger lightly on the string. Keeping your finger there, a student should measure the distance from the head, where the tuning pegs are, to your finger. Everyone should write this measurement down, then divide it into the length of the whole string. They will discover that it is exactly one half the length—a ratio of one to two.

The note you are playing is called the first or lowest harmonic. Now look for the second harmonic, the second lowest harmonic. Plucking with one finger, move the other finger gradually away from the head until the next harmonic rings out. Measure this and do the division again. The second harmonic rings at a ratio of two to three. The third harmonic will have a ratio of three to four. See if the students can find the pattern to determine the next harmonic ratios. Another stringed instrument like a violin or bass can be used.

Next, see if students can match each ratio with a note in the scale—there are eight notes in the scale which we can number one through eight, with one and eight being the same note, an octave apart. Here is what they will find:

Open string: 1st note of scale—The ratio is 1/1
1st harmonic: 8th or 1st note of scale (higher)—The ratio is 1/2
2nd harmonic: 5th note of scale—The ratio is 2/3
3rd harmonic: 8th or 1st note of scale (high)—The ratio is 3/4
4th harmonic: 3rd note of scale—The ratio is 4/5

You end up with three notes, 1, 3, and 5. These notes form a chord called a *triad*.

Build your own marimba! Here's a simple wood-working project using two-by-fours and dowels. Cut four two-by-fours with identical thicknesses and materials (pine or spruce), into pieces according to the above ratios. If the first piece is two meters long, the next one should be cut at ⅘ that length, the next should be cut at ¾, and so on. Save the shorter pieces. You can add them to your scale at ratios of ⅗, ¼, and ⅓. Cut the wood dowels to create hand-held mallets. You have just made a marimba! To make the wood ring well, suspend the pieces above the floor somehow. An old hose or a thick rope works well. Children can have fun playing melodies on their homemade marimba. They can paint the ratios on each piece of wood. You can also use metal pipes. Ask for half-inch wall conduit pipe, otherwise known as Electro-Metallic Tubing (EMT). Start with sections about 36 cm long.

Another musical math activity requires a clock or watch with a second hand. (A metronome would be nice too, but it's not necessary.) If a pulse beats sixty times every minute, how fast is that? How fast is one hundred and twenty pulses per minute? How about ninety? Children can tap one per second, then two, and so on. This will help them to count and understand musical timing. These are great musical math problems.

Music Enhances Science Studies

A mother came to pick up her daughter at the end of the day. The mother asked, "What did you do today?" The child said, "Oh, we used our voices to make sand dance." The mother replied, "Sand can't dance." The child said simply, "Oh Mom, you need to go back to school."

Here's a fascinating scientific experiment. You need:

- a drum head such as a bass or snare drum (or a piece of sheet metal with edges filed smooth so they won't snag anyone, or a sheet of glass with taped edges)
- some dry sand
- a microphone
- an amplifier and speaker

Connect the amplifier to the speaker on the floor, facing up. Place the drum head on top of the speaker, with some air in between. Place some dry sand on top of the drum. Now sing into the microphone and see how the sound makes the sand resonate.

The fascinating part of this experiment is that you can actually make shapes in the sand, depending on what vowels you sing, how high or low the note is, and whether you're singing with a nasal or muddy voice.

Let the students experiment with their voices. Avoid screaming. It's chaotic, and the sand tends to explode all over the place. Have them sing various vowels. Because it is a scientific experiment, they should keep a record of the results. A male teacher singing a low nasal "Oo" vowel can actually create a perfect circle in the sand. Students will discover that they can create parallel lines as well as dots within circles.

When J.J. sings an Oo vowel on a high note, the sand makes a _____ shape. (Draw shape)

When J.J. sings an Oo vowel on a low note, the sand makes a _____ shape. (Draw shape)

When R.L. sings an Oo vowel on a high note, the sand makes a _____ shape. (Draw shape)

When R.L. sings an Oo vowel on a low note, the sand makes a _____ shape. (Draw shape)

Do the same with different vowels. Always try to sustain the note.

Music and biology relate, too. Ever wonder why we want to move and dance when we hear rock and roll? Play some rock and roll through the speakers and watch the sand dance. We dance for the same reason. It's an automatic reaction. (Plus the fact that exciting music makes our adrenaline pump up, and we immediately entrain to the rhythm and dance.)

Sound studies. Remember the word *timbre*? It refers to the quality of sound each instrument and voice has. The timbre or tone quality of a violin is different than the timbre of a flute. Every material that can resonate makes a sound. Scientists have been studying sound ever since Pythagoras two thousand years ago. Your class can do scientific studies of sound also.

Find ordinary objects in the classroom like rulers, pieces of paper, and pencils. Explore the different timbres that each of these make. Divide the class into groups and give each group an object. Ask each group to list twenty different timbres they can create with that object. A wooden ruler, as discussed before, can create many different timbres. One hand can hold it at the end of the desk and the other can pluck it, creating a delightful *boiiing* sound. You can rub it against a desk, tie a string to it, and wave it through the air. The faster you wave it, the higher the sound. The possibilities are numerous.

Explore various objects in a similar way—objects made of wood, plastic, glass, paper, cardboard, metal, cloth, water, and stone. Ask a group to discover fifty different sounds they can make using only their hands, a piece of paper, or a cooking pot.

Next explore the notion of resonance. Something has to vibrate in order for sound to be created. What is vibrating? Strings vibrate on stringed instruments. Wind instruments like trumpets produce sound by sending vibrations through the air inside the instrument. The vibration is caused by buzzing lips against the mouthpiece. Percussion instruments like drums vibrate when struck, thus making the air inside and around them vibrate.

As they study timbres or how different materials make different sounds, students can also study how different sounds, when combined together, create completely new sounds. These sounds are called musical textures. Students can experiment combining timbres; for example, crumple paper and wave it in the air quickly.

An enjoyable way to study both timbre and texture is to create sound effects. Using kitchen utensils and objects found around the classroom, create the following sound effects: a door opening, an arrow flying through the air, an arrow hitting a tree, wind, rain, thunder, a busy intersection, someone walking, and a rocket ship. For example, a clipboard *snap* combined with a ruler *boiiiing* could sound like an arrow hitting a tree. Stick some tape onto a desk. As you slowly pull the tape off, have someone else slowly rip some paper. The combined sound is of someone ripping his or her pants.

Record a pencil being sharpened in a mechanical sharpener while others shuffle their desks. It can sound like a rocket taking off. There is no limit to the sound effects students can create. Listen to old radio dramas like Orson Welles' "The War of the Worlds." Invite students to make up their own radio play using the sound effects they have invented.

Synthesized sound is a whole new field of music study. Completely new timbres can be created. The sound of a jet taking off can become the timbre for a melody. Sounds mixing the diverse timbres of anvils, violins, and crying babies can be created. In addition, the computers connected to these synthesizers can be programmed to play entire symphonies. Science classes can invite scientists in to show what a sound wave is, how it sounds, and how changing the shape of the wave changes the timbre.

How do we hear? The vibration has to change four times before we hear it. Symbolically, the vibration passes through air, earth, water, and fire—meaning air, the eardrum and hammer/stirrups, the water of the cochlea, and the fire of the electrical nerve signal to the brain. But we also hear through bone conduction. Block your ears with your hands and hum. The sound travels through bone to reach your ear. Since sound is made of vibration, our skin and organs can also "hear" vibrations or sound.

DIALOGUE

Here are some questions for you and your students:

How sensitive are you to the sounds around you? Can you detect the rhythms and speeds in your students' speech?

_____

_____

Can you hear the hum of electric appliances? (B♭) What sounds do you block out?

_____

_____

Music Enhances Social Studies

The study of diverse cultures is fascinating, especially when that culture comes alive through its celebration—through its music. Every culture approaches music in a different way. The act of consciously making sounds is universal, but the concept of music, as understood in the Western world, is not.

For example, in parts of West Africa, there is no word for music—and yet it is everywhere. When people work, they sing. Public places are filled with street musicians. Children at play sing and dance. If they are tending the garden, they sing. Traditionally a *griot* or professional musician stands on the side of the field and plays instruments. Without these human-made sounds, it is believed, the garden won't grow. The sounds have a living force. There is no concept of audience in this culture. Everyone present is involved with making the music, whether they are singing along or dancing. The act of making the music is an act of generosity—when you sing and play instruments, you are giving to your brothers and sisters.

These concepts differ from the Western world's concept of music. You cannot assume that musical concepts like performer or audience, or music as an art form, are universal. They are not.

It would be impossible to understand a culture and the way the people in that culture think without first understanding how they identify themselves and what gives them power. Music and the arts help provide a cultural identity which gives people a sense of belonging—a sense of power. When children study the music of diverse cultures, they often learn more about the music of their own culture.

When studying the music of a culture, there are certain key questions you must ask.

- Who makes music?
- How do children learn music in the culture?
- What is the purpose of music?
- When do they make music?
- What instruments do they play?
- What languages do they sing in?
- What is their style of singing? Is it nasal? breathy? low? chanted?
- Is the music allowed to change?
- Is the music written down or learned orally?
- Is new music still composed?
- Does dance accompany the music?
- Is there sacred music? Are there rules about the music as to where, when, and by whom it can be performed?

When children study the music of diverse cultures, they often learn more about the music of their own culture.

Besides discussing all of these questions with students, there are other musical activities you can do to teach cultural awareness. Music publishers have met the strong demand for multicultural music materials. There are now many songbooks, tapes, and videos on hundreds of cultures, even very specific ones, like songs of the Hmong people of Cambodia. See the list of music publishers on page 66. Many organizations are of great help. I strongly recommend both World Music Press and World Music at West publishers as sources of multicultural materials.

S H O P T A L K

Sadie, Stanley, ed. *The New Grove Dictionary of Music and Musicians*. London: Macmillan, 1988.

This dictionary is a wonderful resource containing extensive information on cultural music. This is a superb encyclopedia of all the music on this planet, including the history of the music in each culture as well as descriptions and illustrations of the instruments of each culture. It's well worth the trip to the library.

```
DIALOGUE

Which music of a certain culture and time would I like to
explore with my students?

_____

What is the purpose of music in that culture? How is music
taught?

_____

Is the music oral or written? Can you tell if it comes from a
classical, folk, or popular tradition?

_____

Does the music use elements from the music of other cultures?
Why do you think this is? (For example, some of the popular
dance music of a group within the Navajo Nation borrows from
the Polish polka tradition. Elements of Spanish flámenco music
can be found in the contemporary music of Thailand.)

_____
```

Making instruments. Children love to make musical instruments. Use oatmeal boxes with varnished burlap covers to make drums. Soft drink containers filled with buttons, beads, or gravel become shakers. Rubber bands wrapped around a shoebox become stringed instruments. Milk containers can become guitars. Large soft drink bottles become violins. A clay flower pot, a break drum, and a jelly mold become a bell symphony. When painted in traditional styles, you have a thing of beauty. For example, use the Native American designs shown in *How To Make Drums, Tomtoms, and Rattles* by Bernard S. Mason (1974). The children in many of the world's cultures make similar imitation instruments as their natural way of learning.

Here's a mysterious instrument that is easy to make. Using the metal tray from your oven, take two wires (copper or other) and securely tie one to each end of the tray so they can hang freely in a vertical position. Wrap your forefingers around the ends of the wires, then place your forefingers in your ears so that the tray hangs below you (you have to bend over a little bit). Now have someone gently knock the oven tray chimes with a wooden spoon or other object. A whole range of colorful sounds suddenly fill your head. No one else hears this except you.

You can produce similar instruments using metal hangers. Trust me, these are amazing!

SHOPTALK

Mason, Bernard S. *How To Make Drums, Tomtoms, and Rattles*. New York: Dover Publications, 1974.

If you want to learn some near-authentic ways of making Native American drums, including soaking and stretching the skins, this is the book for you. It includes a guide to painting the drums with designs from diverse Native Nations. Please note: some Native American groups feel that the making of drums should be reserved for Indians only. I feel, however, that if you make it clear that you are not making sacred medicine drums, then you can study the tradition without intruding on it. See also the book, *Moving Within the Circle: Contemporary Native American Music and Dance* by Bryan Burton.

Sawyer, David. *Vibrations: Making Unorthodox Musical Instruments*. New York: Cambridge University Press, 1978.

This book describes some very imaginative instruments. Some, like the whirling friction drum, are a hit with elementary schoolchildren.

If you're going to go to the trouble of making drums, bells, and other instruments, play them as well—in fact, play them often. I visited fifth grade students in Watertown, Massachusetts, off and on over the period of a year. At the beginning of the year, they built their own percussion instruments, drums, rattles, rasps, xylophones, and bells. Almost every day, their teachers would find the time to do a few minutes of drumming. I'm convinced that the drumming helped the students in many ways. It enhanced their rhythms of learning, giving them better attention during study times. The sound and rhythms charged their bodies and minds. And the act of making music together brought them together as a community. They began the year doing simple

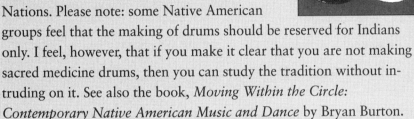

unison beats to accompany songs. By the end of the year, they were able to create fairly complicated rhythmic patterns, including different rhythms simultaneously.

There are many resources on building instruments with children. Using simple tools like hammers, hand saws, hand drills, glue, and elbow grease, you can make all kinds of instruments—instruments where the air vibrates, a string vibrates, the lip vibrates, a skin like a drumhead vibrates, or an object like a piece of metal or wood vibrates. All acoustic instruments fall into these categories.

Do you want to involve your students in a study of culture? Invite them to invent a culture. Where would they live? What would they believe? Based on these things, students can then create the instruments that people in their invented culture play. For example, imagine an entire civilization that lives in supermarkets. They might play zucchini flutes, coconut castanets, kitchen-utensil percussion, tin can drums, and washtub bass violins.

Music can be used to teach a general understanding of historical time and place.

Music Enhances Geography

Using the names of capital cities, write a simple rap or spoken round, for example:

Albany and Boston and Sacramento.

Springfield, Pierre, Philadelphia, Juneau

and so on.

Take an imaginary musical journey using the song, "The Wheels on the Bus." Everyone boards an imaginary bus which then stops in different ethnic neighborhoods in the city. Sing a song from that culture like a Chinese American folksong. Then get back on the bus, singing another verse of "The Wheels on the Bus." Children can learn Italian American, Irish American, African American, Mexican American and many other American songs. And on the journey they can learn about each other. (Note: Italian American songs don't necessarily have to be in Italian. Swedish Americans sing the Italian song "Santa Lucia" at Christmas.)

The challenge with this particular project is that communities don't sing the way they used to. So when you ask someone from a Russian American community for a song, they might not have one or it might be the same song sung in the Irish, Italian, and Chinese neighborhoods. As I said before, we are all more multicultural than we realize.

How To Use Music in Teaching History

Music enhances social studies and can be used to teach a general understanding of historical time and place. For example, to study the people of the Smoky Mountain region of North Carolina in the 1820s, you would ask the same questions listed on page 39. There are three cultural groups you would examine—the people of the Cherokee Nation; the white settlers, those both deeply rooted and those newly immigrated; and the African population who were enslaved.

You might want to study the instruments that each culture played, or their musical habits like country dances attended by both white settlers and Cherokee, or the religious services attended separately by all three groups. You might look into the types of songs they sang in their homes and communities. Did they sing as they worked?

Remember, at this time there were no tape recorders. It's not possible to fully understand the music simply by listening to tapes. Singing the songs in the traditional manner is the most powerful way to create a feeling for the people and who they were.

It would be impossible to recreate exactly what they sang. The music of all three cultures was primarily folk music—music from the oral tradition, not written down. Until the 1870s, for example, hymn books consisted only of words. The melodies could change from community to community.

But you don't need to recreate the exact songs in order to recreate the feel for the time and place. You can recreate a community or family sing-along using a mix of traditional and contemporary songs. There are numerous songbooks and recordings available on the songs and music of all three cultures. For example, to find songs reflecting the African American slave culture, try children's play songs from *Step It Down—Games, Plays, Songs and Stories from the Afro-American Heritage* by Bessie Jones and Bess Lomax Hawes (1987). Or sample African American worksongs and folksongs in *Ain't You Got a Right to the Tree of Life? The People of St. John's Island, South Carolina—Their Faces, Their Words, and Their Songs* by Guy and Candie Carawan (1989).

Historic events. Sometimes you can find old music textbooks in dusty school storage rooms. Often these books have songs arranged to coincide with historic events like the conquest of the American West, the Great Depression, and military conflicts like the Civil War. Using these books, it's easy to attach songs like "Home on the Range," "Pennies from Heaven," and "Battle Hymn of the Republic" to their respective historic events. Each is a great song, but even more important, each song says a lot about the historic event from which it originates.

While learning about the westward movement from the perspectives of both the settlers and the native peoples, teach the song "Home on the Range," originally titled "My Western Home" written in 1873. The wonderful song expresses a love for the prairie.

Home on the Range
by Brewster Higley and Dan Kelly

Verse 1   O give me a home where the buffalo roam
           Where the deer and the antelope play,
           Where seldom is heard a discouraging word
           And the skies are not cloudy all day.

Chorus   Home, home on the range,
           Where the deer and the antelope play
           Where seldom is heard a discouraging word
           And the skies are not cloudy all day.

Verse 2   Where the air is so pure and the zephyrs so free
           And the breezes so balmy and light,
           That I would not exchange my home on the range
           For all the cities so bright
           (chorus)

Verse 3   How often at night when the heavens are bright
           With the light of the glittering stars,
           I stand there amazed and I ask as I gaze,
           "Does their glory exceed that of ours?"
           (chorus)

Write the song in big letters on a large piece of paper. If your students keep notebooks, ask them to copy the words into their notebooks. Help them learn the song. Then as a preparation for discussion, ask them to list five phrases from the song that reflect the settlers' attitudes toward western expansion.

Now teach the contemporary Native American song, "I Walk With Beauty Before Me." The song is based on a Navajo poem, "Now I Walk in Beauty." To understand the song, you must understand the Navajo concept of beauty. To oversimplify, *beauty* refers to the interdependent balance in all of nature. This balance is seen as a harmony of all things. The tree is in harmony with the air, which is in harmony with the water and the earth. To walk in beauty is to walk in harmony with nature.

Your students can learn and write the song and the poem into their notebooks. As before, they can then list five things about the song and poem that tell how the Navajos feel about the land and world around them.

If you want, you could then list the similarities and differences between the songs "Home on the Range" and "I Walk With Beauty Before Me."

I Walk With Beauty Before Me
Contemporary Native American

I walk with beau-ty be-fore me.   I walk with beau-ty be-

hind me.   I walk with beau-ty a-bove me.

I walk with beau-ty be-hind me.   Your world is so beau-ti-ful O

God.

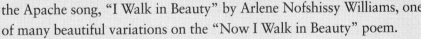

S H O P T A L K

Burton, Bryan. *Moving Within the Circle: Contemporary Native American Music and Dance*. Danbury, Connecticut: World Music Press, 1993.

This exciting book with accompanying tape and slides presents several songs from diverse Native American traditions. The book includes the Apache song, "I Walk in Beauty" by Arlene Nofshissy Williams, one of many beautiful variations on the "Now I Walk in Beauty" poem.

The songs we sing help to define who we are. And sometimes, it is the songs themselves that help to shape our history.

By now, you may see how effective songs are as historical records of how people behaved and thought. Songs help to reinforce cultural identity. The songs we sing help to define who we are. And sometimes, it is the songs themselves that help to shape our history.

Show your students a segment of the video *Eyes on the Prize*, the award-winning documentary on the Civil Rights movement. Ask them how often people sang in the video. They will realize that there is singing throughout, that songs helped to define the movement. When people marched, they sang. When people were locked up in jail, they sang. The singing reinforced their identity as freedom fighters, and it solidified their powerful sense of community. Have the students sing "Ain't Gonna' Let Nobody Turn Me 'Round" or "Woke Up This Mornin' With My Mind Stayed on Freedom." Songs like these breathe life into history. Through songs, students come to know the excitement and passion of the times.

We are talking here of songs that helped to change the world—Union songs like "Union Maid" and "Solidarity Forever"; Zionist songs like "Vine and Fig Tree"; women's rights songs like "Bread and Roses"; anthems like France's "La Marseillaise" and South Africa's "N'Kosi Sikeleli Africa" (Bless, Oh Lord, Our Country Africa); and the Mexican American workers song, "De Colores." These songs are all a part of the history from which they originate. Remove the songs, and the history would change.

Many songs are inspired by historical events—songs like "The Ship Titanic" or the old campaign song "Tippecanoe and Tyler Too." *Sing Out! The Folksong Magazine* gives excellent historical backgrounds to the songs (see Chapter 5, page 68). For example, if you are studying the history of transportation in the United States, there are many canal, sailing, railroad, and highway songs to choose from. Students could make a transportation songbook or present an assembly where the audience tours the United States in several imagined modes of transportation using the appropriate songs.

Songs breathe life into history. Through songs, students come to know the excitement and passion of the times.

Your students can contribute to the historical tradition. They can write original words and music, or they can do what happens most often with historical songs—they can change the words to an existing song. Civil rights songs and Union songs were often based on spirituals. Before the age of copyright laws, borrowing other peoples' music was a common folk practice, as common as borrowing the design for folk furniture. Use the five steps outlined in the songwriting section, and add a step—discuss the song and its relevance to the historical event it describes.

DIALOGUE

What changes have occurred in the way students listen? Are they more attentive after music activities? Are their attention spans affected? Is there any change in students' confidence levels?

_____

_____

_____

Is my confidence as a teacher growing? Do I feel more at ease using music in the classroom?

_____

_____

Chapter 4

A Simple Guide to Teaching Songs

There was once a boy in one of my classes who hated to sing. He'd tell me flat out, "I hate to sing." But everyone in the class would be singing away and through the corner of my eye, I could see he loved to sing.

Learning new songs can be exciting. The trick is to foster as much confidence in your students as possible. To do this, it is often necessary to teach new songs very slowly, using careful repetitions within a supportive environment. The support for singing must come from both teacher and class. Nothing inhibits a child like a negative comment from you or a peer. Remember that everyone can sing well and that everyone can sing in tune if they sing songs within their range, listen closely to the notes, and if they believe they can learn.

Your Class Should Sound Great

Choose songs that your group will enjoy singing. Every age group is different, but common sense says that the song for the younger child should be easier to sing than the song for the older child. This means easy words, easy melody, catchy rhythms, and a small vocal range (not too high or low). The more repetition, the better, especially with the younger child. Songs like "This Little Light of Mine" have plenty of repetition, and will sound great sung by just about any age group.

Don't think of your class as a chorus that has to stand perfectly still. Use movement all the time. Move your fingers. Move your hands and arms. Move your toes and feet and legs. Move your whole body. Even simple movements like lifting the eyebrows make a difference in the singing. (It lifts the palette, creating a brighter sound.)

Once your students have learned a song, sing it often, but don't let the students tire of it. Remind them to sound good. No one enjoys singing in a mushy way. Because song learning is important to the overall learning process, keep teaching new songs.

Because every song is different, every song will need a slightly different teaching strategy. Also, every child learns differently—some are visually oriented, some aurally, some are kinetic, and some prefer symbols or a combination of the above. Generally, the more senses you involve in all of your teaching, the more effective your teaching will be.

The more senses you involve in all of your teaching, the more effective your teaching will be.

DIALOGUE

Which stage are my students at?

☐ can sustain a steady beat

☐ can play instruments with a steady beat

☐ can sing together

☐ can sing and play instruments

☐ can sing in tune

☐ can sing rounds (like "Row, Row, Row Your Boat")

☐ can sing in harmony

What are my immediate goals to enhance their abilities?

_____

_____

_____

_____

_____

_____

_____

SHOPTALK

Page, Nick. *Sing and Shine On! Powerful Song Leading for a Multicultural, Multiple Intelligence World.* Portsmouth, New Hampshire: Heinemann, 1995.

This is an in-depth book for classroom teachers on how to bring powerful song teaching to your school. The book combines an explanation of both the multicultural and multiple

intelligence perspectives for teaching songs with the effect of music on the body and mind. At the end of the book are 65 reasons why singing and music should be central to education.

The Call-and-Response Song

The easiest song to teach and lead is the call-and-response song. You sing a phrase and your students echo it. The trick is to keep a steady beat going while you do it.

Ella Jenkins' song "Jambo" is a good example of a call-and-response song. The Swahili words say "Hello." The first syllable of "Jambo" is pronounced "jahm" as in the word John, not as in the word jam.

Jambo

Jambo

Leader:	Jambo
Group:	Jambo
Leader:	Jambo sana jambo
Group:	Jambo sana jambo
Leader:	Hello
Group:	Hello
Leader:	Hello, friends, hello
Group:	Hello, friends, hello.

The leader keeps the song going, substituting the word "friends" with *watoto*, meaning "children" or using the names of the children, "Hello, Michael, hello."

Sometimes, folksongs can be turned into call-and-response songs.

The Water Is Wide

English Folksong

The wa-ter is wide   I can-not cross o-ver

and nei-ther have I   wings to fly   give me a   boat

that can car-ry   two   and both shall row   my love   and I

The Water Is Wide (Waly Waly)

Leader:	The water is wide
Group:	The water is wide
Leader:	I cannot cross o'er
Group:	I cannot cross o'er

and so on.

You can create call-and-response songs spontaneously. I know a kindergarten teacher who used to struggle to get the children to put things away and come sit in a circle. Then she began singing simple call-and-response phrases on simple melodies like the "Na Na" melody children use to taunt each other. (It's called a descending minor third and it is the easiest melody for young children to sing.)

Leader: (sung) Put away our crayons.
Group: Put away our crayons. (They would immediately respond.)

Leader: Put away our paper.
Group: Put away our paper.

Leader: Come join the circle.
Group: Come join the circle.

and so on.

The teacher would simply sing the instructions rather than speaking them, and the students would echo and respond. The teacher was not composing a great symphony, she was simply singing her instructions in a call-and-response way. It is very effective.

You can use the call-and-response technique with clapping and instruments as well. It's also fun to go around the circle sometimes and have students clap four beat patterns that the class then echoes.

For example =clap, =rest, =faster claps (8th notes)

Leader:

Group:

Leader:

Group:

Leader:

Group:

Leader:

Group:

Be sure to keep a steady beat going. Don't stop the beat between rhythms. You can make up your own rhythms varying the claps with knee taps, shoulder taps, and head taps.

From clapping, move to spoken repetition. For example:

Leader: How are you?

Group: How are you?

Leader: I'm fine.

Group: I'm fine.

You can follow this with a call-and-response exercise where you speak the rhythm, and they clap it back. For example:

Leader: How are you? Are you well?

Group:

Leader: I feel great, I hope you're well.

Group:

The next two call-and-response activities involve the use of simple percussion instruments like drums, or any instrument or object that is hit by a mallet or a stick. Shakers don't work as well because the sound tends to come after the motion which throws off the rhythm. Students without instruments can tap their thighs or desks with their hands. Simply do as before, except have the students echo with their instruments instead of with their voices or with clapping.

When the students can do all of these call-and-response activities well, then you are ready to compose simple instrumental pieces where more than one rhythm is used at the same time. By using contrasting rhythms based on spoken phrases, you can build interesting textures.

For example, those with sticks repeat this pattern.

Denver, Boston, and East L.A.

Add to that the drums repeating.

New York, Philadelphia

Add the bells repeating.

Saint Louis, Kansas City

Students struggling with math or science problems can use the call-and-response technique to learn everything from math tables to the studies of dinosaurs. (See *Raps and Rhymes in Maths* by Ann and Johnny Baker, 1991.)

Leader: Five times seven is thirty-five.
Group: Five times seven is thirty-five.

Leader: Five times eight is forty.
Group: Five time eight is forty.

Students may learn their multiplication table faster this way than through basic rote repetition. Speaking of rote repetition...

The Rote Technique

If you have a song that uses two or more word phrases but not more than four or six, the basic rote technique may work the best. Let's use the beautiful African American spiritual, "My Lord, What a Morning."

My Lord, What a Morning

African American spiritual

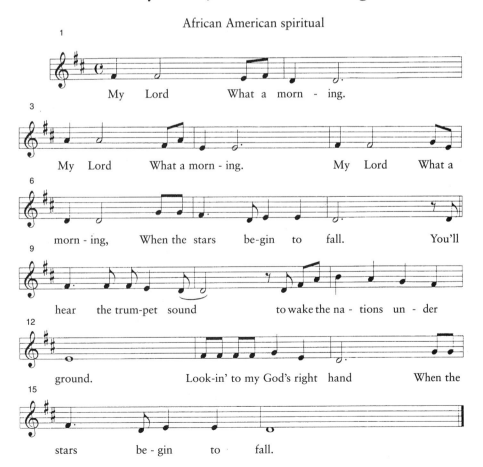

My Lord, What a Morning

Chorus	My Lord, what a morning, (3x)
	When the stars begin to fall.
Verse 1	You'll hear the trumpet sound
	To wake the nations underground
	Lookin' to my God's right hand
	When the stars begin to fall.
	(chorus)
Verse 2	You'll hear the sinner mourn
	To wake... (Same as Verse 1)
	(chorus)
Verse 3	You'll hear the Christian shout...
	To wake... (Same as Verse 1)
	(chorus)

Step 1. Introduce the song, explaining anything you can about where it comes from and why the song is interesting. Even the most common of songs have some background. With songs steeped in cultural traditions like spirituals, there are an abundance of topics to discuss. The more we know about the cultural background of a song, the more powerful the song becomes. In the case of the spiritual, "My Lord, What a Morning," it is a song filled with wonder, probably telling of a comet or large falling star. Some believe that it refers to a Biblical event like the star that followed Jesus—an astronomical event of Biblical proportions, an event that would "wake the nations underground." The Christian faith is at the heart of most spirituals. Note: Schools that avoid religious songs should still consider using spirituals because of their inherent link to cultural identities. (See *The Spirituals and the Blues, An Interpretation* by James H. Cone, 1972.)

Step 2. Perform the song with enthusiasm. It's good for students to hear an immediate model of what they are going to sing. Sing in a normal voice. An operatic voice may intimidate students. Also sing the song in an accessible range (not too high or low).

Step 3. As in the call-and-response technique, break the song up into short phrases, having students repeat each phrase after you. If the words are tricky or in a different language, begin with speaking the words only. Explain the meaning of difficult words. It's important to keep a steady beat going. The chorus to "My Lord, What a Morning" is repetitive, and therefore easier to learn. Students can usually pick it up after hearing it sung a few times. We'll break up the first verse.

Leader: You'll hear the trumpet sound

Group: You'll hear the trumpet sound

Leader: To wake the nations underground

Group: To wake the nations underground

and so on.

If a mistake is made, simply repeat the fragment without disrupting the pulse.

Step 4. Keep the pulse going, gradually asking the class to repeat longer and longer phrases. Usually more repetition is better than less.

Leader: You'll hear the trumpet sound
To wake the nations underground

Group: You'll hear the trumpet sound
To wake the nations underground

Step 5. Once you feel your students know the phrases well, have them put the whole verse together. Remember not to do too much. This technique does not work as well with longer songs. Also be aware that you don't have to learn every song right away—you can learn it over a period of sessions. It is important, however, that whatever students learn in each session, they learn it well and they sound good singing it. When the singing doesn't sound good, students may lose their confidence and desire to sing.

As a rule, the best way to know if a class knows a song well is to have them sing it by themselves without you singing along. For this reason, avoid using piano, guitars, or tapes as accompaniment. Children should learn to sing without any aids to help them.

Multisensory Techniques

Remember that the more senses we use, the better we learn. Hand signs, movements, drawings, photographs, and word sheets, therefore, are powerful tools for learning songs.

Hand signs. Let's imagine a song with words like, "I live in a square house. The square is in a circle. The circle is a spiral, and my square is there." Instead of spending five minutes learning this through the rote technique, these words can be taught in a flash through movement and song. Have the class imitate your motions while you fashion a square in the air followed by another square then a circle, then a circle, a spiral, and a pointing gesture at the end. Do all this silently, then do it again singing the song. They imitate the hand signs again, but don't sing. Finally, have students sing the song and do the gestures. That's it! In a few moments, they have learned the song.

Hand signs are easy to make up. Children can invent their own hand signs for songs. Go back and sing "The Water Is Wide" (on page 50) using made up hand signs. Combining call-and-response songs with hand signs is very effective and lots of fun.

Dance and movement. Songs that involve dancing, like party game songs, are easy to learn. The song "Old King Glory on the Mountain" practically teaches itself when combined with the dance.

Everyone stands in a circle, holding hands. The leader sings the simple song once through.

Old King Glory on the Mountain

Old King Glo - ry on the moun - tain, the moun-tain was so high, it near-ly touched the sky and the first one the sec-ond one the third fol - low me.

The leader sings it again, this time walking around the circle counter-clockwise. On the words, "And the first one," tap the head of the person you are passing, and then the next two people on the words, "The second one, the third follow me." The third person, now three people behind you, becomes the new leader. You continue the game, inviting everyone to join in singing. All will easily follow.

As with all singing activities, it's important that students sing the song well, even a game song.

The music must always sound great. It's easy to do—simply make gentle corrections and give supportive suggestions.

Children can improvise movements to accompany a song or instrumental piece. In a spacious area, begin the song and ask what motions might look good with the music. Students will contribute ideas, everyone begins moving, and you're off. It is enormously entertaining.

The opposite is also true. Teach a song and ask the students to do completely unrelated movements. For a lullaby, ask them to jump up and down. For an action song, ask them to stand still, moving only their eyebrows up and down. This technique, known as *isolation*, invites students to concentrate on one activity while doing something completely contrary. It enhances the students' concentration abilities. Whatever they are learning will become ingrained in their memory because of the concentration they give while learning it. It's amazing and it's true. Even the simple act of snapping fingers, clapping, or tapping the thigh adds beneficial movements to a song and makes the process of learning songs easier.

Drawings and photographs. Like hand signs, images of objects are a tremendous aid in learning songs. This is particularly true for younger children. The children will enjoy illustrating songs. They can even draw music that has no words. Play a recording and ask them to draw the images that come to mind. This can be an enlightening exercise.

Word sheets. Word sheets are excellent for song teaching. Children learn to read as they learn the song. Every class should have an easel with newsprint and markers. Having students look up toward a mounted word sheet is better than having them looking down at hand-held sheets or books. With mounted word sheets, their heads are up, which creates better singing; and you can see who is having difficulty with the words. You can decorate large song sheets and mount them on the walls or store them for another time.

Children at all levels can make their own songbooks by recording the words to the songs they learn in class and collecting them in simple three-ring notebooks or manila folders. This contributes to their sense of ownership of the music and is a wonderful writing exercise. As with all learning activities, the multisensory techniques are extremely effective. They can be used with both the rote and call-and-response techniques.

Teaching Rounds

Rounds like "Row, Row, Row Your Boat" are great for children to sing because they require advanced listening skills. Anything that advances listening advances learning. The children must be able to listen to another part while singing their own. The resulting harmonies are exciting, and students will gain self-confidence as they succeed at such a challenging task. The trick is to help them sound good. Here's how.

Teach the round using one of the techniques mentioned before. When you think students know it well, have them sing it by themselves. It's important that they sing without your support. If they can't sing the song without your singing along, then the round will probably fall apart. Students can become accustomed to singing only what the teacher sings. Since you can only sing one part of a round at a time, the students may become confused.

Once they know the song, ask them to concentrate and sing soft enough so that they can hear each other well. Singing loudly never works with rounds as they simply can't hear the other parts.

Divide the group into two equal parts. Never try the round in more than two groups until students can handle two parts. Sing the round through twice with everyone, without stopping between repetitions. At the end of the second repetition, give a stop hand signal to the group that shouldn't sing. Without breaking the rhythm, signal the other group to begin the round again. When it's time for the second group to enter, give them a clear signal to start. When the first group has finished the round, cue them to start again. Similarly, cue the second group the second time around. When group one has come to the end again, simply give them the stop hand sign, doing likewise to the second group in turn. If the round falls apart, that's okay. Sing it a few more times in unison. It is usually the rhythm that needs work—students are singing too fast or pausing between phrases.

Once they can sing it in two parts, ask your students if they are ready to try it in three or more parts. When singing rounds, have the students sing softly, with a steady pulse, and without you backing them up with instruments or with your voice.

```
                    D I A L O G U E

Ask your students to answer these questions (and try answer-
ing them yourself).

What did I learn from this music activity? What did this song
teach me?

_____

How does making music make me feel? Do some songs affect
me more than others? Which ones? Why?

_____

Has anything I learned from music helped me in my other subjects?

_____

What risks did I take in making music?

_____
```

Teaching Children To Sing in Tune

If you sing songs within a comfortable range (not too high and not too low), children will most likely learn to sing in tune naturally. The ideal range for children is generally from middle C up to G. When children are asked to sing songs that are too high or too low, or songs with difficult melodies, they will have difficulty matching pitches. Children who sing out of tune do not have problems with their voices—there are simply notes they don't hear well. If they can hear a note, then they can sing the note. It's that simple. They reproduce what they hear, and if their hearing is fuzzy, then their intonation will be fuzzy. (The word *intonation* refers to singing in tune.)

If a song is not being sung in tune, fix it. When children are taught to sing in tune, it becomes easier for them to hear and repeat notes correctly. In a class of thirty, as many as twenty children may have trouble hearing the pitches at first. Careful listening over time works wonders with those twenty students.

If you teach songs for the first time with upper elementary students, especially if they haven't sung much, your biggest obstacle will be poor intonation. Help them learn to sing in tune. It takes only a few moments to set the class on the right track. Taking the time will be very worthwhile in the end.

The technique is simple. It involves inner hearing—hearing sounds inside the head. Choose one of the first notes in a song they are having trouble with. Sing that note on an "Oo" vowel and ask the class to hear the note in their heads. Repeat the note if necessary. Then ask the students to sing the note.

It is rare that the class cannot match the pitch. Make sure the note you choose isn't too high or too low for their voices. Your comfortable voice range may not be your students' most comfortable range. If you sing too low or too high, you may have a reverse effect on the students—you may actually be teaching them how to sing out of tune.

Start the song again, making sure they can hear their starting notes in their heads. It's amazing how effective this technique is. If you stick with it, you'll get what you ask for.

Male teachers may not want to use their voices as models for students to listen to as their voices may be too low for some students. The male teacher can simply ask one of the students to sing the "Oo" vowel. That student then becomes the model. Everyone can sing in tune. Students must first learn to hear the notes in their heads.

If things don't go well the first time you teach a song, if the students react negatively or if they simply can't learn it, do not despair. These things happen even with the most experienced song leaders. Be confident that the students can sing well, given time.

Doing music with children, whether singing songs or playing with percussion instruments or computers, is not a difficult task. It is as effortless as breathing, talking, and moving. The benefits are amazing. We become amazing. Like the boy mentioned in Chapter 2, it's fun being ten feet tall.

Field Notes: Teacher-To-Teacher

Often a group of students singing for the first time will be very bashful. They will giggle a lot and look around to see if anyone else is singing. I don't get angry with them. I simply smile and say, "Do you know how amazing you are going to sound in a few moments?" We then sing some more, getting the body involved. They become more and more excited. I do some call-and-response songs, real easy material. They are beginning to sound good. We do a dance song and suddenly, they aren't thinking about it any more—they are simply doing it. Finally, when they are sounding good, I tell them so. They need to hear this. We all need to hear this.

–NP

Periodically, you'll want to stop, reflect on, and assess your students' musical progress. These questions may help:

- How do my students improve their singing? (Do they feel more confident? Is their intonation improving? Are they singing out more? Are they energized by the songs?)
- Can students find something to relate to in the music? (Are they able to make connections between the songs and music and the other subjects they are studying?)
- Are students gaining a sense of musical ownership? Do they feel free to make the folksongs their own, for example, and to make changes to suit their needs or creative whims?
- Which students learn better through musical activities? Is there a change with students who had disciplinary problems?
- Has group music-making affected their sense of community? Has it affected their ability to work as a group?

D I A L O G U E

What steps will I take to break down any inhibitions or fears my students have about making music, especially singing?

_____

_____

_____

_____

_____

_____

Final Thoughts—Yes to Music

Yes to music. Yes to music in every classroom. Yes to music coming from the voices and bodies of every student in every school. Yes to minds learning at accelerated rates because of music and the arts. Yes to academic scores going through the roof. Yes to students working together in a newfound harmony.

Remember the Navajo philosophy, *to walk in beauty*. It refers to their belief that all parts of nature, including human beings, are in balance with each other—they are in harmony with each other. To walk in beauty is to walk in harmony with all things.

Too many of our children in the United States walk in a kind of ugliness. They sense neither balance nor harmony around them. Many of them are labeled as being poor students or disciplinary problems. The bright star within them is not allowed to shine. They walk in an ugliness not of their own invention.

As educators, we have the responsibility to guide students on their paths without leading them. Each child ultimately chooses his or her own path. What we can do is to ensure that the path be one of beauty, not ugliness. By creating learning environments where creativity is part of human intelligence, where social skills are essential for learning, where dance, music, and all the arts are integral to the identity of student, classroom, and school, we create an academic balance that is truly healthy—a balance based on the harmony of body, mind, spirit, and community. In such an environment, students can walk in beauty on their paths to being powerful human beings, active citizens, and responsible contributors to the ongoing creative unfolding of life on this planet.

SHOPTALK

Choksy, Lois. *The Kodaly Context: Creating an Environment for Musical Learning*. Old Tappan, New Jersey: Prentice Hall, 1981. The Kodaly Context refers to class singing with an emphasis on *solfège*, the system of singing and music reading based on pitch and rhythm vocables like do, re, mi, and ti-ti tiri-tiri ta. Some of this book is intended for the music specialist.

Sing Out! The Folksong Magazine. P.O. Box 5253, Bethlehem, Pennsylvania 18015-5253. This is a magazine started by Pete Seeger in the 1950s dedicated to folk music and musicians. They also publish songbooks and tapes including the superb songbook *Rise Up Singing!*

Chapter 5
Where To Find Songs

You can learn songs from children, from your colleagues, from recordings, and from songbooks. The more songs you know, the better, but you always have to start with one song. Here are some rousing fun or moving songs, and songbooks. See page 66 for a list of music publishers.

From the songbook *Rise Up Singing* (with tapes) published by Sing Out Corporation

"Baby Beluga" by Raffi and D. Pike

"Bread and Roses" (women's rights anthem), words by James Oppenheim, original music by Caroline Kohsleet, new music by Mimi Fariña

"De Colores" (United Farm Workers folksong)

"Had I a Golden Thread" by Pete Seeger

"If I Had a Hammer" by Pete Seeger and Lee Hays

"Donna Donna" (Yiddish Theater Song), words by Aaron Zeitlin, music by Sholem Secunda, translation by Arthur Kevess and Teddi Schwartz

"Follow the Drinking Gourd" (African American folksong)

"Garden Song" by David Mallet

"Go Down Moses" (spiritual)

"Good Night Irene" by Leadbelly (Huddie Ledbetter)

"Green Grow the Rushes" (English folksong)

"Harriet Tubman" by Walter Robinson

"Hava Nagila" (Hebrew round)

"Home on the Range" (folksong)

"Jig Along Home" by Woody Guthrie

"Let It Be" by John Lennon and Paul McCartney

"The Midnight Special" by Leadbelly (Huddie Ledbetter)

"My Lord, What a Morning" (spiritual)

"Never Turning Back" by Pat Humphries

"River" by Bill Staines

"Roll On Columbia" by Woody Guthrie

"Simple Gifts" (Shaker hymn)

"The Ship Titanic" (traditional)

"Solidarity Forever," words by Ralph Chaplin

"Swing Low Sweet Chariot" (spiritual)

"This Land Is Your Land" by Woody Guthrie

"This Little Light of Mine" (spiritual)

"Tzena, Tzena" (Hebrew round)

"Union Maid" by Woody Guthrie

"The Water Is Wide (Waly Waly)" (English folksong)

"The Wheels on the Bus" (children's song)

"With a Little Help From My Friends" by John Lennon and Paul McCartney

"Vine and Fig Tree" by Shalom Altman

"Zum Gali Gali" (Israeli round)

From Ysaye Maria Barnwell's and George Brandon's six-tape collection *Singing in the African American Tradition,* **available from Homespun Tapes**

"Ain't Gonna Let Nobody Turn Me 'Round" (civil rights)

"I Feel Like Going On," words by Eleanor D. Bell-Stokes, music by
    Andre Sonny Woods

"Somagwaza" (South African song)

"The Storm Is Passing Over (Courage My Soul)" by Charles Albert Tindley

"Wade in the Water" (spiritual)

"Woke Up This Mornin'" (spiritual/civil rights)

"Woyaya (We'll Get There)" by T. Osei, Sol Amarifio, L. Amao, M. Tonton, W.
    Richardson, R. Bailey, and R. Bedeau (South African)

From recording *All for Freedom* **by Sweet Honey in the Rock, available from Music for Little People or Ladyslipper Catalog**

"Cumbayah"

"Freedom Calypso"

"Ise Oluwah" (Yuroba chant, West Africa)

"Little Red Caboose"

"Make a Little Motion"

"Silvie" by Leadbelly

"So Glad I'm Here"

From *Freedom Is Coming*, ed. by Anders Nyberg, South African songbook and tape, available from Dove Music or World Music West

"Freedom Is Coming"

"Thuma Mina"

"We are Marching"

"We Will Not Give Up the Fight"

From Libana songbooks, available from Ladyslipper Catalog

"The Earth Is Our Mother" (Native American)

"Kwaheri" (from Kenya)

"Neesa Neesa" (Seneca)

"Wearing My Long Wing Feathers" (contemporary Native American)

From *Fireside Book of Folk Songs* by Margaret Bradford Boni, published by Simon and Schuster

"Battle Hymn of the Republic," words by Julia Ward Howe, melody based on
    "John Brown's Body"

"La Marseillaise (1792)" by Rouget de Lisle

Other Songs Mentioned in *Music as a Way of Knowing*

"All Work Together" by Woody Guthrie, available from Sing Out Corporation

"Bless Oh Lord Our Country Africa" by Enoch Sontonga Octavo, available
    from World Music Press (N'Kosi Sikeleli Afrika, Anthem of the ANC, and
    now all of South Africa)

"Bridges" from Bill Staines' *First Million Miles,* available from Rounder
    Records

"Do–Re–Mi" from *The Sound of Music* by Rodgers and Hammerstein

"Earth Angel" from *The Doo-Wop Songbook*

"Happy Birthday to You," words by Patty Smith Hill, music by Mildred J.
    Hill (1893)

"I Walk in Beauty" by Arlene Nofshissy Williams, from *Moving Within the
    Circle* by Bryon Burton, available from World Music Press

"Jambo" by Ella Jenkins, from *The Ella Jenkins Songbook*

"Pennies From Heaven" by Burke and Johnson, published by Campbell Connelly

"Old King Glory on the Mountain" from *The Christmas Revels Songbook,*
    edited by Nancy and Jack Langstaff

"Sweet Honey in the Rock" from *Compositions: One* by Bernice Johnson
    Reagon, available from Ladyslipper Catalog

"There Is More Love," recorded on Bernice Johnson Reagon's *River of Life,*
    available from Ladyslipper Catalog

"Tippecanoe and Tyler Too," words by Alexander C. Ross (1840), available as "Harrison Song" from *Music for Patriots*

"Tumbalaika" from the Harvard Hillel Sabbath Songbook, available from Tara Publications

"Yonder Come Day," available from World Music Press

Music Publishers

Alexander Publishing
3537 Old Conejo Road, Suite 101
Newberry Park, California 91320
They publish manuals giving simple explanations on how to use the many MIDI systems and electric pianos.

Canyon Records
4143 N. 16th Street
Phoenix, Arizona 85016
This is an excellent source for Native American music, especially Navajo.

Computers and Music
647 Mission Street
San Francisco, California 94105
This quarterly catalog of current software and hardware, both Macintosh and IBM, includes educational materials.

Dekay's House of Music
39 Thrift Street
San Francisco, California 94112
Dekay's is a black gospel music distributor of recordings, octavos, and songbooks. They also have how-to books on gospel style piano playing.

Dove Music
P.O. Box 08286
Milwaukee, Wisconsin 53208
This multicultural music catalog concentrates on Spanish American music.

Dr. T's
220 Boylston Street, Suite 206
Chestnut Hill, Massachusetts 02167
Dr. T's is a reliable creator of Atari and Amiga music software.

Homespun Tapes
P.O. Box 694
Woodstock, New York 12498
This company produces how-to tapes and videos on learning folk and jazz instruments, tapes on yodeling, singing in harmony, and Ysaye Maria Barnwell's and George Brandon's exceptional set, *Singing in the African American Tradition.*

Honey Rock
RD 4, Box 87
Everett, Pennsylvania 15537
Honey Rock distributes multicultural percussion-related materials for performers and music educators, including how to purchase drums from around the world.

Institute for Music, Health, and Education
Don G. Campbell, Director
P.O. Box 1244
Boulder, Colorado 80306
This organization is dedicated to the research of listening and its uses in health and education. They distribute many books and tapes including information on accelerated learning.

Ladyslipper Catalog
P.O. Box 3124-R
Durham, North Carolina 27715
This catalog of recordings, videos, and books is dedicated to women's music including music of diverse cultures.

Maestro Music, Inc.
2403 San Mateo NE P-12
Albuquerque, New Mexico 87110
This music theory software for Apple II is aimed at grades 1-12 as a support to music specialists—how to read and understand music.

Micro Music, Inc.
5353 Buford Highway
Atlanta, Georgia 30340
A retailer of music hardware and software, they sell a book that reviews available music software, *The Musical PC* by MIDI America.

Music Educators National Conference (MENC)
1902 Association Drive
Reston, Virginia 22091
MENC publishes a monthly magazine and many instructional books for music educators, both instrumental and choral.

Music for Little People
P.O. Box 1460
Redway, California 95560
The Music for Little People catalog is full of recordings for children and parents.

Music of the World
P.O. Box 3620
Chapel Hill, North Carolina 27505
This catalog includes recordings from many cultures.

OPCODE, New Tools For Education
3950 Fabian Way
Palo Alto, California 94303
OPCODE is a distributor of music education software.

Sing Out Corporation
P.O. Box 5253
Bethlehem, Pennsylvania 18015
Sing Out! The Folksong Magazine, started by Pete Seeger in the 1950s, is dedicated to folk music and musicians. They also publish songbooks and tapes including the superb songbook, *Rise Up Singing!*

Tara Publications
29 Derby Avenue
Cedarhurst, New York 11516
This is an excellent source for traditional and contemporary Jewish music of all kinds including music for children.

World Around Songs
Route 5 Box 398
Burnsville, North Carolina 28714
Since the 1950s, these songbook pamphlets have been wonderful resources for music of many cultures.

World Music at West
Multicultural Music and Arts Catalog
1208 5th Street
Coralville, Iowa 52241
This catalog contains world music resources for teachers.

World Music Press
Judith Cook Tucker, Publisher
P.O. Box 2563
Danbury, Connecticut 06813
Judith Cook Tucker is an ethnomusicologist dedicated to helping teachers bring diverse music into the schools. Her songbooks with tapes and her choral arrangements are practical, authentic, and very easy to use.

Zephyr Press
3316 N. Chapel Avenue
P.O. Box 66006-P
Tucson, Arizona 85728
Zephyr Press publishes education guidebooks that deal with all aspects of multisensory learning.

Professional Bibliography

Amsco Publications. *Rounds for Children*. New York: Amsco Publications, 1986. This is a good collection of rounds for ages 5-12.

Arc Music and Hal Leonard Publishing. *The Doo-Wop Songbook*. New York: Arc Music and Hal Leonard Publishing, 1989. The collection contains piano chords, and vocal only—there are few harmony parts.

Baker, Ann and Johnny Baker. *Raps and Rhymes in Maths*. Portsmouth, New Hampshire: Heinemann, 1991. This fun collection of rhythm math activities helps teachers address many areas of math in the primary grades.

Barnwell, Ysaye Maria and George Brandon. *Singing in the African American Tradition: Choral and Congregational Vocal Music*. Woodstock, New York: Homespun Tapes, 1989. This excellent set contains six tapes by Sweet Honey in the Rock member Ysaye Barnwell, who teaches the songs. Most are for singers capable of singing in four-part harmonies.

Blood-Patterson, Peter, ed. *Rise Up Singing*. Bethlehem, Pennsylvania: Sing Out Corporation, 1988. *Rise Up Singing* is the best collection of folksong lyrics around. Tapes are available.

Boody, Charles G. *TIPS: Technology for Music Educators*. Reston, Virginia: Music Educators National Conference (MENC), 1990. This is a good source for electronic activities for the classroom.

Bradford Boni, Margaret, ed. *Fireside Book of Folk Songs*. New York: Simon and Schuster, 1947. You'll find wonderful arrangements of great songs.

Brewer, Chris and Don G. Campbell. *Rhythms of Learning: Creative Tools for Developing Lifelong Skills.* Tucson, Arizona: Zephyr Press, 1991. The authors present interesting views on rhythm and how to use rhythmic awareness in teaching. The book discusses subjects like entrainment.

Bridges, Lois. *Assessment: Continuous Learning.* Strategies for Teaching and Learning Professional Library, The Galef Institute. York, Maine: Stenhouse Publishers, 1995. See how authentic assessment invites teachers to find out what children know, how they can use what they know to learn, and what they can teach us. The author provides kidwatching and assessment forms that have been recommended by a variety of classroom teachers.

_____. *Creating Your Classroom Community.* Strategies for Teaching and Learning Professional Library, The Galef Institute. York, Maine: Stenhouse Publishers, 1995. Reading lofts, learning centers, student art, and more create an atmosphere where children want to learn.

Brodsky Lawrence, Vera. *Music for Patriots, Politicians, and Presidents, Harmonies and Discords of the First Hundred Years.* New York: Macmillan, 1975. This book contains the song "Tippecanoe and Tyler Too," among others.

Brubeck, Dave. *Take Five* (recording). Columbia Records, JCS 9116. *Take Five* contains the jazz piece "Blue Rondo à la Turk."

Burton, Bryan. *Moving Within the Circle: Contemporary Native American Music and Dance.* Danbury, Connecticut: World Music Press, 1993. This excellent collection for teachers includes a tape and slides. It dispels the old stereotypes about Native American music.

Campbell, Don G. *One Hundred Ways To Improve Teaching Using Your Voice and Music, Pathways to Accelerated Learning.* Tucson, Arizona: Zephyr Press, 1992. Some useful ideas on the use of music in accelerated learning are presented here.

Cantril, Hadley. *The Invasion from Mars, A Study in the Psychology of Panic With the Complete Script of the Famous Orson Welles Broadcast.* Princeton, New Jersey: Princeton University Press, 1940, 1982. This work contains the radio adaptation of Orson Welles' "War of the Worlds."

Carawan, Guy and Candie Carawan. *Ain't You Got a Right to the Tree of Life? The People of St. John's Island, South Carolina—Their Faces, Their Words, and Their Songs.* Athens, Georgia: The University of Georgia Press, 1989. Pick up this book for a fascinating look at a fascinating culture.

_____. *Sing for Freedom, The Story of the Civil Rights Movement Through Its Songs.* Bethlehem, Pennsylvania: Sing Out Corporation, 1990. This excellent resource shows how songs convey historical information.

Carpenter, Robert A. *Technology in the Music Classroom.* Van Nuys, California: Alfred Publishing, 1991. This is an interesting resource for teachers who want to incorporate music technology in their classrooms.

Choksy, Lois. *The Kodaly Context: Creating an Environment for Musical Learning.* Old Tappan, New Jersey: Prentice Hall, 1981. The Kodaly Context refers to the system of singing and music reading based on pitch and rhythm vocables. Some of this book is intended for the music specialist.

Cline, Dallas. *Homemade Instruments.* New York: Music Sales, 1976. You'll have fun making your own instruments.

Cone, James H. *The Spirituals and the Blues, An Interpretation.* Maryknoll, New York: Orbis Books, 1972. If you had thought of spirituals and blues as being happy music, this book will show you otherwise.

Fink, Cathy, Marcy Marxer, Robin Williams and Linda Williams. *Learn To Sing Harmony.* Woodstock, New York: Homespun Tapes, 1986. Audiotapes with booklet. *Learn To Sing Harmony* is good for the beginner, although it's no substitute to joining a chorus or folksong group.

Fogelquist, Mark and Patricia Harpole. *Los Mariachis! An Introduction to the Mariachi Tradition of Mexico.* Danbury, Connecticut: World Music Press, 1989. A teacher-friendly book and tape presents the exciting tradition of Mexican American mariachis.

Gardner, Howard. *Frames of Mind: The Theory of Multiple Intelligences.* New York: Basic Books, 1983. Gardner explains the many facets of intelligence.

Gold, Ben-Zion. *Harvard Hillel Sabbath Songbook, One Hundred Sabbath Songs with All the Sabbath Blessings.* Boston: David R. Godine, 1992. This is a wonderful collection of sacred songs.

Hampton, Henry, producer. *Eyes on the Prize* (video series). PBS and the New Learning Project. Alexandria, Virginia: Public Broadcasting Service, 1987. There is an educators' package available for this award-winning TV series on the Civil Rights movement.

Heller, Paul G. *Drama as a Way of Knowing.* Strategies for Teaching and Learning Professional Library, The Galef Institute. York, Maine: Stenhouse Publishers, 1995. Learn how improvisation, pantomime, scriptwriting, research, and acting are tools for learning.

Hopkins, Jerry. *How To Make Your Own Hawaiian Musical Instruments.* Honolulu: Bess Press, 1988. Expand your study of culture by learning to make these fun Hawaiian instruments.

Jenkins, Ella. *The Ella Jenkins Songbook.* New York: Oak Publications, 1968. This is an excellent collection of children's songs from many cultures.

_____. *This Is Rhythm*. Bethlehem, Pennsylvania: Sing Out Corporation, 1993. A fun children's songbook (with tape) explores rhythm instruments with twelve songs from many cultures—illustrations by Garrian Manning.

Jones, Bessie and Bess Lomax Hawes. *Step It Down—Games, Plays, Songs and Stories from the Afro-American Heritage*. Athens, Georgia: University of Georgia Press, 1987. Kids can learn great games with wonderful historical explanations for the songs and the play-song traditions.

Jones, Quincy. *Back on the Block* (recording). Burbank, California: Qwest Records, 1989. The best of contemporary rap, jazz, and soul are combined in this exciting recording.

Langstaff, Nancy and John Langstaff, eds. *The Christmas Revels Songbook: In Celebration of the Winter Solstice*. Boston: David R. Godine, 1985. It includes Wassail songs and other seasonal songs.

Lazear, David. *Seven Pathways of Learning: Teaching Students and Parents about Multiple Intelligences*. Tucson, Arizona: Zephyr Press, 1994. This is one of four excellent books by Lazear using Howard Gardner's approach to multiple intelligences.

Makeba, Miriam. "Umam' Uyajabula." *Sangoma*, track 17. Warner Brothers Records, catalog no. 9-25673-2, 1988. Miriam Makeba sings a South African homecoming song from captivity to freedom, "I am delighted that I'm going home."

Mason, Bernard S. *How To Make Drums, Tomtoms, and Rattles*. New York: Dover Publications, 1974. If you want to learn some near-authentic ways of making Native American drums, this is the book for you. It includes a guide to painting the drums with designs from diverse Native Nations.

Nash, Grace C. and Janice Rapley. *Music in the Making: Optimal Learning in Speech, Song, Instrument Instruction, and Movement for Grades K-4*. Van Nuys, California: Alfred Publishing, 1990. Grace Nash revolutionized music education during the 50s and 60s. Her books on counting and reading rhythm games are excellent for the classroom teacher. Look for *Do It My Way: The Child's Way of Learning* and *Creative Approaches To Child Development*, both published by Alfred Publishing.

Nguyen, Phong and Patricia Shehan Campbell. *From Rice Paddies and Temple Yards: Traditional Music of Vietnam*. Danbury, Connecticut: World Music Press, 1991. Book and tape. There is a lot to learn from the old world music of Vietnam.

Nyberg, Anders, ed. *Freedom Is Coming: Songs of Protest and Praise from South Africa*. Chapel Hill, North Carolina: Walton Music Corporation. 1984. (Available from World Music Press.) This is an excellent collection of exciting songs from South Africa (with tape).

Oates, Eddie. *Making Musical Instruments*. New York: HarperCollins Children's Books, 1995. You'll learn how to make a variety of instruments.

Ohanian, Susan. *Math as a Way of Knowing*, Strategies for Teaching and Learning Professional Library, The Galef Institute. York, Maine: Stenhouse Publishers, 1995. Classroom examples demonstrate how students learn real world math by thinking, talking, listening, negotiating, and writing.

Page, Nick. *Sing and Shine On! Powerful Song Leading for a Multicultural, Multiple Intelligence World*. Portsmouth, New Hampshire: Heinemann, 1995. The author explains why singing is essential as well as how to teach powerful singing in the classroom. Nick Page does teacher workshops and school sing-alongs using songs from many cultures. He can be contacted at 135 Highland #2, Winthrop, Massachusetts 02152-1541.

Rauscher, Frances H., Gordon L. Shaw, and Katherine N. Ky. "Music and Spatial Task Performance," *Nature,* October 1993. Researchers find that college students listening to Mozart increase their short-term spatial reasoning.

Rauscher, Frances H., Gordon L. Shaw, Linda J. Levine, Katherine N. Ky, and Eric L. Wright. "Music and Spatial Task Performance: A Causal Relationship." Paper presented at the American Psychological Association 102nd Annual Convention, Los Angeles, August 1994. Researchers find that music study increases spatial reasoning among three year olds.

Rollins, Susan, ed. *A Circle Is Cast*. Cambridge, Massachusetts: Libana, 1986. A collection of songbooks and tapes by a Boston-based women's chorus.

_____. *Fire Within*. Cambridge, Massachusetts: Libana, 1990. *Fire Within* contains great chants and rounds from many traditions.

Sadie, Stanley, ed. *The New Grove Dictionary of Music and Musicians*. London: Macmillan, 1988. This dictionary is an extraordinary multi-volume resource on music from all cultures.

Sawyer, David. *Vibrations: Making Unorthodox Musical Instruments*. New York: Cambridge University Press, 1978. With this book you can make creative instruments, like the whirling friction drum.

Seeger, Pete. *Abiyoyo*. New York: Macmillan, 1985. This is an illustrated children's story adapted by Pete Seeger. Children can sing along with the song "Abiyoyo" as the book is read to them. Delightful!

_____. *Where Have All the Flowers Gone: A Singer's Stories, Songs, Seeds, Robberies*. Bethlehem, Pennsylvania: Sing Out Corporation, 1983. Pete Seeger uses his songs and others to tell his life story. Captivating!

Seeger, Ruth Crawford. *American Folk Songs for Children: In Home, School and Nursery School*. New York: Doubleday, 1948. This is a classic song collection for children.

Shehan Campbell, Patricia, Ellen McCullough-Brabson and Judith Cook Tucker. *Roots and Branches: A Legacy of Multicultural Music for Children.* Danbury, Connecticut: World Music Press, 1994. An invaluable book and tape or CD for the teacher who wants to teach songs of many cultures.

Sleeter, Christine E. and Carl A. Grant. *Making Choices for Multicultural Education: Five Approaches to Race, Class, and Gender.* Columbus, Ohio: Merrill Publishing, 1988. A history of the multicultural movement in education from rising African American awareness to the current movement towards inclusiveness and the democratization of education.

Staines, Bill. *If I Were a Word, Then I'd Be a Song.* Sharon, Connecticut: Folk-Legacy Records, 1980. The songbook includes "All God's Critters Got a Place in the Choir," and "River."

_____. *First Million Miles* (recording). Cambridge, Massachusetts: Rounder Records, 1989. Staines's album contains many great songs.

Stanley, Lawrence A., ed. *Rap, the Lyrics: The Words to Rap's Greatest Hits.* New York: Penguin Books, 1992. From urban poetry to angry political statements, this collection of rap lyrics is a valuable source for anyone who wants to know more about rap. Understanding leads to appreciation.

Sweet Honey in the Rock. *All for Freedom.* (recording) Redway, California: Music For Little People, 1989. *All for Freedom* contains great African and African American songs for children.

Tomatis, Alfred A. *The Conscious Ear, My Life of Transformation Through Listening.* Barrytown, New York: Station Hill Press, 1991. Tomatis offers controversial methodology concerning the ear in learning and healing.

Toop, David. *Rap Attack 2: African Rap to Global Hip Hop.* London: Serpent's Tail, 1991. The history of rap music from its African roots to its Jamaican and New York merger to its final commercialization.

Walther, Tom. *Make Mine Music.* New York: Little, Brown, Brown Paper School Books, 1981. This illustrated book suggests activities for making instruments for ages 13 and up.

Warring, Dennis. *Making Wood Folk Instruments.* New York: Sterling Publishing, 1990. This is a fun instrument-making book for all ages.

Wiggins, Jackie. *Composition in the Classroom: A Tool for Teaching.* Reston, Virginia: Music Educators National Conference (MENC), 1991. Fun compositions by young students add depth to this good how-to book.

_____. *Synthesizers in the Elementary Music Classroom: An Integrated Approach.* Reston, Virginia: Music Educators National Conference (MENC), 1991. If your school has Atari or Amiga computers, this is a good resource to have. Both computers were designed for excellent music use.

Professional Associations and Publications

The American Alliance for Health, Physical Education, Recreation, and Dance (AAHPERD)
Journal of Physical Education, Recreation, and Dance
1900 Association Drive
Reston, Virginia 22091

American Alliance for Theater and Education (AATE)
AATE Newsletter
c/o Arizona State University Theater Department
Box 873411
Tempe, Arizona 85287

American Association for the Advancement of Science (AAAS)
Science Magazine
1333 H Street NW
Washington, DC 20005

American Association of Colleges for Teacher Education (AACTE)
AACTE Briefs
1 DuPont Circle NW, Suite 610
Washington, DC 20036

American Association of School Administrators (AASA)
The School Administrator
1801 North Moore Street
Arlington, Virginia 22209

Association for Childhood Education International (ACEI)
Childhood Education: Infancy Through Early Adolescence
11141 Georgia Avenue, Suite 200
Wheaton, Maryland 20902

Association for Supervision and Curriculum Development (ASCD)
Educational Leadership
1250 North Pitt Street
Alexandria, Virginia 22314

The Council for Exceptional Children (CEC)
Teaching Exceptional Children
1920 Association Drive
Reston, Virginia 22091

Education Theater Association (ETA)
Dramatics
3368 Central Parkway
Cincinnati, Ohio 45225

International Reading Association
(IRA)
The Reading Teacher
800 Barksdale Road
Newark, Delaware 19714

Music Educators National Conference
(MENC)
Music Educators Journal
1806 Robert Fulton Drive
Reston, Virginia 22091

National Art Education Association
(NAEA)
Art Education
1916 Association Drive
Reston, Virginia 22091

National Association for the Education
of Young Children (NAEYC)
Young Children
1509 16th Street NW
Washington, DC 20036

National Association of Elementary
School Principals (NAESP)
Communicator
1615 Duke Street
Alexandria, Virginia 22314

National Center for Restructuring
Education, Schools, and Teaching
(NCREST)
Resources for Restructuring
P.O. Box 110
Teachers College, Columbia University
New York, New York 10027

National Council for the Social Studies
(NCSS)
Social Education
Social Studies and the Young Learner
3501 Newark Street NW
Washington, DC 20016

National Council of Supervisors of
Mathematics (NCSM)
*NCSM Newsletter Leadership in
Mathematics Education*
P.O. Box 10667
Golden, Colorado 80401

National Council of Teachers of
English (NCTE)
Language Arts
Primary Voices K-6
1111 Kenyon Road
Urbana, Illinois 61801

National Council of Teachers of
Mathematics (NCTM)
Arithmetic Teacher
Teaching Children Mathematics
1906 Association Drive
Reston, Virginia 22091

National Dance Association
(NDA)
Spotlight on Dance
1900 Association Drive
Reston, Virginia 22091

National Science Teachers Association
(NSTA)
Science and Children
Science for Children: Resources for Teachers
1840 Wilson Boulevard
Arlington, Virginia 22201

Phi Delta Kappa
Phi Delta Kappan
408 North Union
Bloomington, Indiana 47402

Society for Research in Music Education
Journal for Research in Music Education
c/o Music Educators National Conference
1806 Robert Fulton Drive
Reston, Virginia 22091

The Southern Poverty Law Center
Teaching Tolerance
400 Washington Avenue
Montgomery, Alabama 36104

Teachers of English to Speakers of Other
Languages (TESOL)
TESOL Newsletter
1600 Cameron Street, Suite 300
Alexandria, Virginia 22314

Other titles in the
Strategies for Teaching and Learning Professional Library

Administrators Supporting School Change
Robert Wortman
1-57110-047-4   paperback

In this fascinating personal account of how a principal can make a difference in the lives of all he touches through his work, noted principal Bob Wortman outlines his own strategies for creating a positive learning environment where everyone feels valued, respected, and can focus on the business of learning.

Fostering a successful school community demands more than a vision and a philosophy. A successful school administrator needs to know how to maintain positive relationships with all members of the school community—parents, students, and teachers. Classroom teachers, site and district administrators, parents, and policymakers will be interested in Bob's mission to create a schoolwide learning community that includes not only the people in the classrooms, but the support personnel, the families, and the community at large.

Assessment Continuous Learning
Lois Bridges
1-57110-048-2   paperback

Effective teaching begins with knowing your students, and assessment is a learning tool that enables you to know them. In this book Lois Bridges gives you a wide range of teacher-developed kidwatching and assessment forms to show different ways you can reflect on children's thinking and work. She offers developmental checklists, student and child interview suggestions, guidelines for using portfolios in your classroom, rubrics, and self-evaluation profiles. Also included are Dialogues that invite reflection, Shoptalks that offer lively reviews of the best and latest professional literature, and Teacher-To-Teacher Field Notes offering tips and experiences from practicing educators.

Lois identifies five perspectives on assessment—monitoring, observing, interacting, analyzing, and reporting—to think about when designing your own assessments. As you continuously evaluate and monitor your students' learning using a variety of assessment tools, you can design instruction and create curriculum that will stretch your students' knowledge and expand their learning worlds.

Creating Your Classroom **Community**
Lois Bridges
1-57110-049-0   paperback

What do you remember of your own elementary schooling experiences? Chances are the teachers you recall are those who really knew and cared for you as an unique individual with special interests, needs, and experiences. Now, as a teacher with your own classroom and students to care for, you'll want to create a classroom environment that supports each student as an individual while drawing the class together as a thriving learning community.

Lois Bridges offers you the basics of effective elementary school teaching: how to construct a curriculum that focuses not only on what you will teach but how you will teach and evaluate it; how to build a sense of community and responsibility among your students; and how to organize your classroom to support learning and to draw on learning resources from parents and the larger community beyond school.

Drama as a Way of Knowing
Paul G. Heller
1-57110-050-4   paperback

Paul Heller is an experienced teacher, playwright, and producer who is passionate about communicating through language, drama, and music. In this engaging book he shows you how to use drama as an effective part of all classroom learning. While making it clear you don't need previous dramatic training or experience, he presents the nuts and bolts of pantomime and improvisation, of writing and acting scenes, even creating and presenting large-scale productions.

Through his Ten-Step Process in which you, the teacher, are the director, he shows what you should do to guide your students through rewarding dramatic experiences. You will see that drama is a wonderful learning tool that enables students to explore multiple dimensions of their thinking and understanding. And not only is drama academically rewarding and beneficial, it's great fun as well!

Math as a Way of Knowing
Susan Ohanian
1-57110-051-2   paperback

Award-winning author Susan Ohanian conducts a lively tour of classrooms around the country where "math time" means stimulating learning experiences. To demonstrate the point that mathematics is an active, ongoing way of perceiving and interacting with the world, she explores teaching mathematical concepts through hands-on activities; writing and talking about what numbers mean; discovering the where and why of math in everyday life; finding that there are often multiple ways to solve the same problem.

Focusing on the NCTM's *Curriculum and Evaluation Standards for School Mathematics*, Susan takes you into classrooms for a firsthand look at exciting ways the standards are implemented through innovative practices. She introduces you to new ways to organize your curriculum and classroom; suggests ways to create meaningful mathematics homework; gives you ideas to connect math across the curriculum; and links the reflective power of writing to support mathematical understanding.

For the nonspecialist in particular, Susan shows that math really is an exciting and powerful tool that students can really understand and apply in their lives.